The Ultimate Passive Income Guide: Latest Reliable & Profitable Business Ideas

Make $10,000/month with Affiliate Marketing, Blogging, Dropshipping, Amazon FBA, and More

Table of Contents

INTRODUCTION 3
CHAPTER 1—A BEGINNER'S PASSIVE INCOME 6
FOUR TYPES OF PASSIVE INCOME 7
FIVE QUICK-START STEPS FOR PASSIVE INCOME 10
FIVE GENIUS MICRO-INVESTING TOOLS 19
CHAPTER 2--DISCOVER SELF-PUBLISHING SUCCESS 24
HOW TO WRITE A BOOK. YOUR ROAD TOWARD MAKING BIG BUCKS IN SELF-PUBLISHING 27
MARKETING YOUR BOOK. TIPS FOR MAXIMIZING YOUR BOOK PROFITS 37
TIPS FOR PUBLISHING AUDIO BOOKS 39
SIX STEPS TOWARD EARNING EXTRA INCOME BY PUBLISHING ONLINE COURSES .. 42
CHAPTER 3--BLOGGING FOR BIG PROFITS 48
THE TRUTH ABOUT EARNING THROUGH BLOGS 48
SEVEN WAYS TO EARN INCOME FROM BLOGGING 54
CHAPTER 4—MAKE PASSIVE INCOME ON THE INTERNET NOW 59
ALL YOU NEED TO KNOW ABOUT AFFILIATE MARKETING 59
FIVE STEPS TOWARD BECOMING AN AFFILIATE MARKETER 61
MAKE MONEY DROPSHIPPING 68
FIVE ESSENTIAL STEPS IN CREATING DROPSHIPPING BUSINESS 69
CHAPTER 5—GET RICHER WHILE YOU SLEEP 73
AMAZON FBA 73
ALL YOU NEED TO KNOW ABOUT PEER-TO-PEER LENDING OPPORTUNITIES .. 75
40 WAYS YOU CAN USE YOUR SKILLS OR INTERESTS TO EARN PASSIVE INCOME . 78
CHAPTER 6--MAKE KILLER INVESTMENTS 86
HOW TO START INVESTING IN STOCKS 86
ALL ABOUT CD LADDERING 91
FOUR SIMPLE WAYS TO MAKE REAL ESTATE INVESTMENT INCOME 92
CONCLUSION 96

Introduction

Let's look into some reasons why you're interested in finding some additional income streams. Maybe you already have a job, but the money you earn from that job never seems to provide enough income to meet all your wants and needs. Or maybe you're making enough income to fulfill your current wants and needs, but you can't imagine working the job you're working now forever. You'd like to transition into a career or careers which offer you more independence, more flexibility, more income, or all of the above. Or maybe you're looking for a way to supplement your current income without spending a lot of time to do so. You're not necessarily looking for "easy money", but it would be nice if you could supplement your income without having to allocate a lot of time to do so.

In this book, I'm going to provide you with the information you'll need to create additional income streams for yourself without having to spend a lot of extra time to do so. You may have heard people boast about making money while they sleep. Well, passive income streams can allow you to do exactly that—make money while you are sleeping. Yes, there will be some initial effort required, but I'll show you some ways to make additional income with minimal effort. In some instances, you'll be able to use your money to make more money. On the other hand, if you don't have the money required to make more money, I'll show you some other ways you can increase your income streams with little or no financial investment. So, if you have the money to make more money, but not the time, I can help you. Likewise, if you have the time but not the money to make more money, I can help you.

My name is David Allen. I call myself a "side hustle" expert. For years, I researched and tried many different ways to create additional income for myself and my family. I've made it my mission in life to find easy and practical ways to make additional income. During my journey, I've developed some tried and true ways for people to make extra income. And yes, I've made some mistakes along the way. But I'm always happy to have others learn from my mistakes and missteps. As I grew older, I've found that my mistakes are fewer and further in between. I'm now at a point where I think I have a lot of good information to share with others. I've proven that I can set up some great passive income streams, many of which require very little time and effort.

In the past, I've imparted many of my findings to friends who were eager to learn how to make more passive income. Many of those friends have benefitted substantially from my knowledge and experience in setting up their own passive income streams. Some of them even credit me for changing their lives; many of them have often encouraged me to write this book and share my vast knowledge with others who are looking to improve their own financial status. I'm hoping that you'll be one of the people who benefit immensely from my knowledge and expertise.

With the information I provide, you will be able to create additional income streams for yourself. You'll be able to earn or save extra money immediately with some of the ideas I provide. Other income streams may take slightly longer, but for the most part, you should be able to start earning extra income without spending a lot of time working on it. As you read this book, you'll note that there are many different means of earning additional income. You'll have to determine which of these income streams will work for you. And once you determine that, you will be well on your way toward earning some additional income through the many different streams available to you.

Since you're reading this book, I'm assuming that you'd probably like to start earning extra income sooner than later. With this in mind, I encourage you to start to change your life now by implementing some of the tips and techniques I'm offering. In writing a self-help book like this, there's always the danger that the reader will subscribe to the ideas offered, but then resolve to implement them later. As we all know, many times, people who resolve to implement the changes later will place the ideas on the back burner and then never get back to them. With this in mind, I'd like to encourage you to start implementing these ideas today. After all, why wait to make changes which will allow you to earn additional income and set you on the road to financial independence? Unless you're independently wealthy, I'm sure you'll be happy to start earning some extra income immediately.

The tips and techniques I provide can yield incredible results, if only you'll take the time to implement them. Every chapter in this book should help you in your efforts to create additional income streams without spending a lot of time in implementing or maintaining these streams. By the time you finish reading this book, you'll know all about passive income streams and how they can change your life. Together, we can make it happen.

Chapter 1—A Beginner's Passive Income

Before I can start telling you how you might start earning passive income, I'd like to first define the term "passive income" and tell you how it is different from other forms of income.

Some of you may have heard the mantra, "Make Money While You Sleep". This concept is often paralleled with the concept of passive income.

Passive income is income resulting from cash flow received on a regular basis—with little or no effort or participation on the part of the recipient. Although I wouldn't classify passive income as "easy money", I'll point out that many passive income streams offer opportunities for people to make money without a lot of effort. Yes, some effort may be required at the outset of any passive income opportunity. However, after that initial effort, many passive income streams allow the recipients to derive income on a continuous basis without a lot of participation, effort, or maintenance.

The U.S. Internal Revenue Service lists three categories of income: active income, passive income, and portfolio income. I'll offer a brief description of each income category so we can keyhole the passive income category we'll be focusing on in this book.

Active income is the income a person earns from standard jobs or a mainstream career. If you're a restaurant waiter, a marketing executive, a nurse, or a teacher...any standard career, the salary you earn in doing that job is considered active income. It's called active income because you are active at earning that income. For example, if you are a restaurant waiter, and you decide not to go to work for a couple of weeks, it's likely that you won't get paid or won't derive any income from that job. You'll only earn income from the job if you are active at it.

You may have heard people previously refer to their main jobs as their "A" jobs and their side venture or side hustle jobs as their "B" jobs. When people refer to their "A" jobs, they are almost always referring to active income jobs in which they derive a steady income resulting from their participation in that career. And many people use the income from their "A" job to get into the two other categories of income—passive income and portfolio income.

Portfolio income is income derived from activities such as investments, dividends, interest, capital gains, and royalties. Portfolio income is not earned through regular business activity. Portfolio income is not derived from passive income investments and is not earned through regular business activity.

Passive income, the type of income we'll be focusing on with this book, is income that is derived regularly from activities that require little or no effort or participation on the part of the recipient. As I've already pointed out, passive income isn't always "easy money" or "money made while sleeping", as many passive income activities require at least some initial effort on the behalf of the person who hopes to benefit. And many passive income activities require some ongoing maintenance to remain successful.

Four Types of Passive Income

Before we start telling you some ways you can earn passive income, let's explain the four types of passive income activities, how they work, and how they are different from each other. Here are the four types of passive income activities:

1) **Use Cash to Buy Cash-Flowing Assets.** This is the "use money to make money" approach. Now, before you get discouraged, we realize that not all of you have the money required to participate in this option. For those of you that don't, other very viable options which don't require cash will follow. But for those of you that have money to use in increasing your assets, you'll be able to do things such as real estate investments, dividend investing, and business lending to increase your passive income earnings. That said, many people who have the "money to make money" find that they don't have the time to put their money to work for them. With this in mind, I'll provide you with some recommendations on how you can use your money to make more money without allocating a lot of extra time to do so.

2) **Build Cash-Flowing Assets.** If you don't have mountains of investable cash available, don't despair. You're not alone. You can still build your passive income earnings. Many people have increased their passive income earnings, spending little or no money. Some have built digital products or websites. Others have developed blogs, comparison shopping concepts, affiliate marketing concepts, or even online teaching courses to create ongoing income streams. Although most of these activities require some initial time and effort, they can provide income streams that will last for a long time, without any upfront expenditures.

3) **Sell or Share Assets.** Do you have assets that you own or control that you can turn into passive income streams? If you'll look around, you can probably identify some tangible assets that could be sold or shared to produce additional income. For example, do you have an exercise bike that you're no longer using and it's just taking up space in your garage? That's an item you could probably sell to earn some

extra income. Do you have a car and some extra time to drive around? If so, you can earn some passive income by becoming an Uber or a Lyft driver. Did you collect baseball cards as a kid? Maybe it's time to sell those cards. Do you have an extra bedroom in your house? Maybe you could rent out that extra room. Do you have an empty shed on your property? Maybe you could rent this shed out as a storage space. In all likelihood, you already have assets there that can be turned into cash. Look around and see what assets you already own or control. You'll almost certainly find that some of these assets can be turned into passive income streams.

4) **Reverse Passive Income.** With this passive income activity, you'll be saving money instead of making money. You'll do so by reducing your ongoing expenses. For example, you could reduce your cable TV bill by renegotiating it or having a negotiating service do that for you. Even if you only negotiate a savings of $20 per month, that will amount to $240 annually. You could also negotiate interest rates on credit cards or switch to credit cards that have better rates or attractive introductory offers. If you are storing some of your belongings in a storage facility, can you get rid of some of the contents of that unit so you can then rent a smaller, less expensive unit? You get the picture...look at your monthly expenses and see if there is a way you could reduce some of those expenses to save money. That's reverse passive income. And even though this activity will not make you more money, it will allow you to save some money that can certainly be used to make more money.

Five Quick-Start Steps for Passive Income

We're going to get going with some ideas for you to start making some quick passive income. Most of the following ideas are offered with the idea that they'll not require a lot of initial startup or setup time. Ideas on more time-intensive passive income streams will follow later in this book. My goal is to get you started immediately with some passive income streams that require very little time. Then, once you realize that you can indeed derive income from these streams, you can proceed to more complex streams that require more startup time.

1) **Credit Cards.** As most people have credit cards, and many of those people use credit cards for their ongoing purchases, let's start with how you can derive passive income from your credit cards.

    There are a number of things you can do with your credit cards to ensure that you get the maximum passive income from those cards.

    The first thing you should consider is the charges that accompany your credit cards. This includes annual fees and interest rates. It's my feeling that you should never pay an annual fee for a credit card that you are using on a regular basis unless the benefits and rewards you receive from having that card substantially outweigh the annual fee. Annual credit card fees will range from $25 to $500 per card. There are plenty credit cards out there that advertise no annual fees and if your credit card company is charging you an annual fee, I suggest that you either consider a switch to another credit card company or call your current credit card company and ask them to waive your annual fee. You should know that almost all credit card companies are open to waiving the annual fees, especially for the first year.

Next, you should find out what the interest rates are on your credit cards and then compare your rate with the rates offered by other credit card companies. If you pay off the full balance on your card every month, the interest rate you get on your card won't matter much, however if you have a continuous balance on that card that you're not able to pay off completely every month, then your interest rate should be a major consideration and you should compare your existing rate with rates offered by other cards. There are many sites on the internet that compare credit card rates, and you should be able to easily compare your rates with other rates with the simple click of a mouse. Again, if your current interest rate is not to your liking but you like your credit card company, you should consider calling your credit card company and asking them to reduce your rate to a more competitive level. Yes, it's possible that they might not accommodate your request, but the worst that can happen is that they say "no". Then if your card rate is not competitive, you can consider switching credit card companies.

Another consideration with credit cards is the benefits or rewards you receive with your card. Does your card offer a cashback program? If so, what is the cashback percentage rate and how does that compare to other cards? Or do you have a travel rewards card? If you do, make sure you plan to utilize the travel miles that are accumulating, before they expire. I've known people who have credit cards with travel rewards that are no longer travelers. For these people, they would be better suited to a credit card that offers rewards other than travel miles. Some credit cards offer gift cards as rewards. Again, you should compare those cards with other cashback or gift card rewards to make sure your credit card company is competitive. If not, consider a switch to another credit card company.

2) **Rewards Programs.** Another way to enhance your earning power is to enroll in rewards programs at places where you regularly shop. For example, my supermarket chain has a rewards program in which I receive periodic discounts on items I purchase and regular discounts on gas purchases at their service station. When I enrolled in this program, I registered online in less than five minutes. I don't have to carry a plastic card in my wallet; I just give them my phone number whenever I make a purchase. On average, I save 20 to 30 cents per gallon at their service station every time I refuel my car. In a similar vein, I buy office supplies for my small business at Office Max, and they also have a rewards program in which all I have to do is give them my phone number whenever I make a purchase. This rewards program accumulates cash rewards that I can use for future purchases.

Also, there are apps such as Drop, which allow people to earn discounts from their top five retailers. You get to choose your favorite retailers and then you accumulate rewards points with each purchase you make from these five retailers. (Even Lyft and Uber are among the businesses you can choose among your five favorites.) The reward points you accumulate can eventually be redeemed as gift cards from major retailers including Amazon, Starbucks, Groupon, etc. Again, registration is simple and free. You'll be registering retailers that you already purchase from, so it's a can't-lose proposition.

3) **Savings Accounts, Checking Accounts.** Most people have checking accounts and some people have savings accounts.

With all of your bank accounts, I suggest that you verify what your interest rates are for those accounts and then compare them with the rates you might receive from other banks. Again, we have to understand that many people choose their banks for convenience reasons. So if the competing banks' interest rates are only slightly higher than that of your bank's, these higher rates may not merit a switch. However, if they are substantially higher, then you might consider a switch or contact your current bank and ask them if they have any other programs that can be made available to you to raise the rates you're receiving. Please know that interest rates on checking accounts are seldom high and you're probably not going to get rich by trying to negotiate rates or switching to another bank. Nevertheless, "a penny saved is a penny earned" and you can decide if a switch or negotiation is worth it.

Just as important in considering your banking expenses are the fees that you'll pay from your bank. As we all know, banks are well-known for fees that are a major source of their revenue and some banks have even been accused of gouging customers with their fees. In evaluating your bank, I strongly suggest that you analyze the fees they charge. Each bank should be able to supply you with a list of fees. Those fees may even be posted on the bank's website. Does your checking account have a monthly maintenance fee? Is there a minimum balance amount before fees are applied? Do you ever have overdrafts? If so, what are their charges? Many banks have overdraft protection programs they can offer you. Many people take these bank charges for granted when it would behoove them to review these charges at least annually to make sure they are competitive with charges and fees from other banks.

Although reviewing, shopping, or negotiating bank fees may not be the most exciting way to make money and may not make you a millionaire, it is something easy that you can do in very little time to make or save you money on a monthly basis.

4) **Certificates of Deposit.** If you're fortunate enough to have enough money to maintain certificates of deposit, I suggest you "shop" interest rates with banks before depositing funds or renewing certificates. As certificates of deposit don't require much attention, it is not unusual for certificate holders to use banks other than their regular banks. Convenience for certificates of deposit is not a factor that it is for checking accounts, as you basically deposit the funds for your certificates of deposit and then the money just stays in the bank for the term of the certificate. So, don't hesitate to shop interest rates with your certificates of deposit.

5) **Rent Your Assets.** Most of us have at least some rentable assets from which we could derive passive income. Do you have a car? A boat? A vacation home? A recreational vehicle? An empty shed or garage stall? A spare room in your home? All of these assets could provide some passive income streams.

   a) **Your house or your spare room.** If you're willing to rent out your house or even a spare room in your house, you can make some serious cash. Airbnb and other similar sites provide reliable vehicles for you to rent out your home. I have friends in Minneapolis that rented out their home for Super Bowl week and, in doing so, they earned enough money to pay their mortgage for an entire year. They earned five figures per night. Yes, they have a nice home, but this will give you an idea of how much money can be raised in renting a house or even a spare room.

Now, it's important to remember that the Super Bowl brings over 100,000 visitors to town and there are not enough hotel rooms to accommodate all the visitors. So, the market is ripe for the picking during that time. Companies like Airbnb will do the background checks on your guests and they will also collect the rental fee you have requested. So, there is very little work on your part except to prepare the home for visitors. My friends who rented out their home for the Super Bowl made arrangements to stay with relatives during the week they had their house rented.

I have another group of friends that similarly rented out their home in a suburb of Minneapolis for the Ryder Cup golf event, which is an international golf event that is extremely popular, almost as popular as the Super Bowl. Likewise, they were able to pay an entire year's mortgage by renting their house to the family of one of the professional golfers participating in the event. Again, what you can rent your home for will depend on the quality of your home and the popularity of the event in your area, but there is substantial money to be made in renting out your home to visitors, whether they are in your city for a major sporting event, a major concert event, a major political convention, etc. Another Minnesota friend of mine rented out his apartment to a member of the news media who was attending the Republican Convention in nearby St. Paul. Again, there were no hotel rooms available and my friend's apartment was on a light-rail train route with easy access to the convention center in St. Paul where the event was being held.

Do you have a vacation home that sits empty for most of the year? I have a lake home on a secluded lake in northern Minnesota. I use that lake home only about five weeks out of every year. With this in mind, I have started renting out this lake home to interested parties. I, of course, block out the periods in which I am going to be using the lake home, but the home is open for rental at all other times. I used a third-party service to manage my bookings, to correspond with the guests, and to do the cleanings before the guests arrive and after they leave. My participation in the entire activity is mostly centered around accepting the money which the management company collects. (Yes, it's a tough job, but someone has to do it!) I've found this to be an extremely profitable side venture and I've noticed that I have a smile on my face every time I deposit one of the checks from this activity.

One more thought on a far more basic level: If you have a spare bedroom or bedrooms in your home that is mostly being used as a junk room, you might consider renting out this room on either a temporary or an ongoing basis. If you do this, you should obviously make sure you vet or do a background check on your prospective renter. You won't want to grant access to your house to a complete stranger. But if you can find a trustworthy person to rent your spare room, it may well be worth the additional income you'll derive from this passive income activity. As an example, I have a family member who has a small spare bedroom in his family's home. They cleaned all of the junk out of their spare bedroom and rented it to a college kid who had a summer internship in their city. Since it was a small bedroom and since their renter was a cash-strapped college kid, the renters didn't get rich from renting the spare bedroom. Nonetheless, they earned some extra income which they appreciated and they convinced the college kid to mow the lawn in the months he was renting.

b) **Your boat or your recreational vehicle.** Along the same lines, if you own a boat or a recreational vehicle (RV), you're probably not using the boat or the RV on a continual basis. In fact, most boat and RV owners use those items only a couple of times a year. These are expensive assets that can be turned into passive revenue streams. Companies such as Boatsetter and GetMyBoat are vehicles in which you can rent out your boat. Companies such as RVShare and Outdoorsy are available for peer-to-peer RV rentals. If you'll browse those sites, you will get a good idea of how much you can rent your boat or RV for. Your boat rental fee will depend on a number of factors, including how large it is and where it is located. Your RV rental fee will depend on similar factors. It is not unusual for an RV rental to bring a $150 to $300 rental per day. Again, the companies that are in this boat rental or RV rental business will often provide the insurance on the boat or the vehicle. At the same time, they will do background checks on the prospective renters and they will collect the rental fee. They'll then take their cut of the action and pay you the remaining amount.

c) **Your car.** The average vehicle sits idle for 22 hours a day. Many families own more than one car. Cars are another asset which you can use to make passive income. Companies such as Turo and Getaround offer peer-to-peer car rental platforms. These companies allow you to set the rental price for your vehicle and, importantly, they handle the vetting for the people who want to rent your car and they also handle the insurance for these rentals.

Another way to use your car as an income stream is to become a driver in your spare time. Most of you are familiar with well-known enterprises such as Uber or Lyft. With these companies, it is a relatively simple process to become accepted as one of their drivers and they offer you the flexibility of driving only when you have the spare time to drive. It's a good way to make extra cash. I have friends who are Uber or Lyft drivers in their spare time and they then use the money they earn to make their monthly car payments or their car insurance payments.

Finally, if you're not picky about what your car looks like, you can opt to make it a mobile billboard. Companies like Wrapify will pay you to use your car as a mobile billboard and to advertise various products or services. The money you make in doing this will depend on where you live (highly-populated areas are preferred) and how many miles you drive. Wrapify and other companies like it will track your mileage and then pay you accordingly. It's not unheard of for people to make $100 a week for their mobile billboards.

Five Genius Micro-Investing Tools

I'll admit that until a couple of years ago, I didn't even know what micro-investing was. For those of you who are not familiar with the concept, I'll give you a quick lesson in what it is and how it works. Micro-investing is an activity in which people can invest small amounts in stock. Micro-investing almost always occurs through mobile platforms or apps. Unlike traditional modes of stock investing, micro-investing is not restricted to people who have lots of money. Investments are often very minimal, as the name micro indicates, and investors can usually invest with as little as $1 to $5 at a time. Micro-investing is designed to remove the traditional roadblocks to investing by beginning investors, including brokerage minimums.

With micro-investing, you will not need to become a stock market wonk. As a matter of fact, you won't need to know anything about the stock market. Most of the micro-investing apps will select portfolios for you, based on your preferences, and then they'll place the small amounts you're investing into those funds. When you first start on a micro-investing app, they'll ask you to fill out a questionnaire so they can determine your preferences and then cater your investments toward your preferences.

One thing I really like about many of the micro-investing apps is that they have automatic means for you to make your small investments. Some of those means are described below under the descriptions of the individual apps.

Although no one would say that you'll become a multi-millionaire by micro-investing and no one would ever proport that you'll become the next Warren Buffett, micro-investing is a good way to get your feet wet in the stock market without laying out or risking a lot of cash. You'll be able to make or save small amounts of money without a major cash outlay and without broker's minimums and fees.

As you might imagine, there are quite a few micro-investing apps to choose from. I'll outline a few of these apps below, but you should note that there are always new apps coming out that you may want to look into if you are interested in micro-investing.

1) **Acorns.** This is one of the most popular apps, as it allows you to invest very small amounts by automatically rounding your debit and credit card charges to the nearest higher dollar amount and then it invests this small extra amount (always less than $1) for you. For example, if I buy a toner cartridge for my printer and the cost of that cartridge is $24.39, Acorns will round the charge up to $25 and add the 61 cents change to my investment account. If for whatever reason, you don't want these amounts invested automatically, you can manually select for which charges these small extra amounts can be invested. The thing I like about this site automatically rounding my charges to the next highest dollar amount is

that I consider these small amounts to be pocket change which will have very little impact on my bank account and which I'm never going to miss. But with all the debit and credit charges I make, those small amounts add up to a decent investment account over a period of time.

To give you an idea as to the amount of money I can save and invest with the Acorns app, I've been averaging over $40 per month saved and invested. Admittedly, I use my debit and credit cards quite frequently, because I use them for personal purchases and for my small business purchases (and I rarely pay cash for the items I purchase), but this will give you an idea as to what you might expect to earn on the Acorns app. I project that my annual savings/investments will total somewhere between $450 and $500 annually. No, that won't put me in the same tax category as Amazon founder Jeff Bezos, but $500 isn't chump change either, at least not for me.

Acorns charges $1 a month for its services, money that I easily get back from my investments. As mentioned before, they'll ask you a few questions when you register with them and they'll use the information you provide to create a financial profile for you. They'll then build your investment portfolio, which can range from conservative to aggressive, depending on the information you give them on your questionnaire.

2) **Stash.** Stash is a bit different than Acorns, as it is slightly more hands-on for investors. With this app, instead of adding to your debit and credit card charges, Stash is set up so you can withdraw a specified amount from your bank account each week or each month. Like Acorns, Stash will ask you a set of questions in an effort to determine whether they should steer you toward conservative, moderate, or

aggressive investments. Once they have determined this, they will provide you with a set of simple portfolios in which you can choose to invest. Again, you'll not need to be a stock expert to determine which stocks you'll invest in, but you'll at least be required to choose a preference, something you won't have to do with Acorns. Stash has a $1 monthly fee and they require that you've accumulated a minimum of $5 before you can start investing.

3) **Rize.** Rize is a goal-oriented savings and investment app. The savings component of this app is designed to help you save the amounts of money you want in order to pay for things you want. For example, if you want to get a new surfboard at a cost of about $400, Rize will set you up on a savings program in which they will designate a specified amount of each of your paychecks toward this purchase. (You'll be the one who specifies the amount to be deducted from each paycheck.) At the same time, you tell them how much money you'll need to purchase a new surfboard, you'll also tell them when you'd like to have this surfboard. With this app, you can easily adjust your settings at any time. You can accelerate or decelerate your payments, if necessary. Rize charges an annual management fee of 0.25% on your investments. Some of these fees are offset by the 1.6% interest they pay on your balance.

4) **Robinhood.** The Robinhood app is an app for buying and selling stocks on U.S. exchanges. The app can also be used to buy and sell ETFs (exchange-traded funds) and cryptocurrencies. This program is well-known because it is free and it doesn't charge any of the fees that are typically associated with stock transactions. No commissions, no account maintenance fees, no trading fees. On the other hand, the Robinhood app is a bare-bones app which does not

offer investment advice or research. If you're interested in buying or selling stocks on this app, you'll have to get your advice elsewhere.

5) **Betterment.** Unlike Robinhood, Betterment allows you to be hands-off with your investments. It also gives you access to financial advisors who can offer investment advice through the app's messaging system. Betterment has two tiers: The Betterment Digital tier is available with no required account minimum. Betterment charges 0.25% of assets for its Digital tier. The company also offers Betterment Premium at 0.40% of assets with a minimum investment of $100,000. With Betterment Premium, the company offers unlimited phone access to members. I realize that Betterment Premium will not be viable to most of us here, but the Betterment Digital tier is a good deal if you are interested to buy and sell stocks and to be able to solicit the advice of their financial advisors throughout the process.

Chapter 2--Discover Self-Publishing Success

Self-publishing is one of the most popular forms of earning passive income. Before I tell you how to discover self-publishing success, I want to make sure you understand what self-publishing is. In the days before the internet, if you wanted to write a book and have it published, you were either totally at the discretion of traditional publishers or you had to pay to have large quantities of your own book printed. Authors who wanted to have their own books printed, probably because they couldn't sell them to publishers, often had to purchase as many as 5000 books in order to get a reasonable price.

In those days, a friend of mine who eventually became a New York Times best-selling author had always had the dream to be an author. After he finished writing his first book, he submitted it to 27 different publishers. He received 27 letters of rejection. He believed in his book and his writing abilities so sincerely that he decided to go the "vanity press" route and have his book printed without a publisher. He had to print 5000 books at that time, and, as a student recently out of college and a person who held a bartending job to pay the bills, he didn't have anything close to the money he needed to print the 5000-book minimum. He was a great salesman and he eventually secured the funds needed through loans from some of his bar patrons.

He had the 5000 books printed and then loaded up the trunk of his car with boxes of his books and drove from bookstore to bookstore in an effort to hawk his books. As I mentioned before, he was a great salesman and he was eventually able to sell all 5000 of his political thriller books to bookstores and individuals. Soon after he reordered his second batch of books, he received a call from a publisher who had been tracking his book purchases from the "vanity press". That publisher asked him to submit a manuscript and soon after that, my friend was offered his first book contract from a publisher. He went on to make a career of it and he wrote six New York Times bestsellers before he, unfortunately, died of cancer at an early age.

I tell you this story of how things used to be so I can illustrate how things have changed since the advent of the internet and digital printers. Now you can write a book, you can load it to an online self-publishing site, and you can sell digital books, printed books, or audiobooks. Most impressively, you can purchase printed books in minimum quantities of one. Yes, you read that right. You can have one book printed at a time. As a matter of fact, with digital printers, your printed book will not be printed until someone orders it online. Then the printer will ship that book within a matter of days, instead of the matter of weeks or months required for printing in the days before the internet.

Although there are quite a few steps involved in writing and self-publishing a book, the process is now so much easier than it ever was before and it can be done very inexpensively. In this book chapter, I'm going to tell you how to write and publish your own books. Publishing your own books is one of the most popular ways for people to earn passive income.

There are a ton of success stories about people who have made a fortune through self-publishing their own books.

Accurate statistics on the book industry aren't always easy to find, but I have some statistics that will show you what a huge market the book market is. According to the NPD Group (National Purchase Diary), a well-known American market research firm, over 696 million printed books were sold in 2018. According to Data Guy, a renowned book industry analyst, over 781 million eBooks were sold from April 2017 through September 2018, totaling a sales amount of $4.02 billion. This should give you a good idea of what you'll be getting into when you decide to self-publish books.

Before we get further along, I should probably define eBooks for those of you who may not be quite sure what the term encompasses. The term eBook is short for electronic book, and it includes all books that can be read on mobile devices such as cell phones and tablets, computers, and eBook devices such as Kindle and Nook.

When you self-publish your books, you are going to have to decide if you want printed books, ebooks, audiobooks, or all of the above. It's very common now for people to publish printed and eBook versions of the same book. Audiobooks are not quite as popular, but they are quickly rising in popularity and they offer yet another vehicle for you to get your book out there for people who prefer listening to books instead of reading them.

Probably the biggest success story in e-publishing is the story of author E.L. James and her *50 Shades of Gray* series. She published her first book in that series in 2011 as an eBook and a print-on-demand paperback. Her books have now sold over a million copies, including books that have now been turned into movies.

Self-publishing success stories are abundant on the internet. I'll take the time to give you one woman's story because it's a great success story and it will give you an idea of the possibilities that self-publishing can offer. Admittedly, very few people will ever achieve these lofty levels, but it's nice to dream, isn't it? Amanda Hocking was an unknown author from Minnesota who couldn't get published by a traditional publisher. She worked a day job as a group home caregiver to pay the bills and then wrote paranormal novels in her spare time. Eventually, she had written 17 books and had a tall pile of rejection letters from publishers and agents, who either didn't believe in her talents or didn't believe that there would be much interest in the genre. Finally, in 2010, frustrated by the publishers and agents who kept rejecting her, Amanda decided to see if she could sell her books on Amazon's Kindle. She self-published her vampire novel, *My Blood Approves,* on Amazon's site. She soon started selling nine books a week on the site. No great shakes, of course, but at least there was some interest, enough interest to prompt her to self-publish three additional books in the series on the site. It wasn't long after posting those three additional books that the series took off. Word obviously got around and from April 2010 through March 2011, she sold over a million copies of nine different books and earned $2 million in sales for those books. At one point, she was selling an average of 9000 books a day. Her sales strategy was brilliant. She sold the first books in her series at only 99 cents in an attempt to get her readers hooked on the series. The subsequent books in the series then sold for $2.99. Some of the conventional publishing houses scoffed at the idea of selling a book for only 99 cents, but Amanda Hocking sold such a huge volume of books that her sales soon put those criticisms to rest. Amanda Hocking is a poster child for the potential of self-publishing.

Now that we have some of the general information and some success stories out of the way, let's get into the nitty-gritty of how to write and publish a book.

How to Write A Book. Your Road Toward Making Big Bucks in Self-Publishing

Find a topic. Before you can write a book, you are going to have to select a subject or a topic. I suggest that you start out with a project that you are interested in. If you can find a topic or niche in which you are interested or passionate, you'll find that you'll enjoy writing the book a lot more. You'll also find that writing a book about something you are knowledgeable or interested in will require a lot less research.

If you don't have a particular subject or niche in mind and just want to write a book to earn extra income, I suggest that you first examine your personal areas of expertise or interest. For example, I have a friend of mine who is an avid biker (bicycle, not motorcycle). A few years ago, he was telling me how he had ridden on every bike trail in the state of Minnesota. He was telling me which trails he really enjoyed, and which trails he only mildly enjoyed. He even told me all about the ice cream shops or the coffee cafes that he would stop in as he traversed these trails. Many of the trails went through small towns that had interesting things to see or hidden gems, such as antique shops, diners, bakeries, or candy shops.

As he was relaying all of this information to me, I finally said, "You know, you should write a book about that. You're a fountain of information on Minnesota bike trails and I think people would be willing to pay for that information." He was taken aback by my idea and brushed it off by saying, "I could never do that. I'm not an author."

I didn't let the subject die and offered to help him self-publish his book if he was willing to gather all of the information. And I'm happy to say that he did publish a book on Minnesota bike trails. Although this book hasn't made him a millionaire, he enjoyed doing it, he is proud that he did it, and he now receives monthly royalty checks from the sales of his book. As a matter of fact, he now uses his bike book sales to fuel his weekend bike trips.

So the moral of the story for those of you who want to write books to earn some extra income: I suggest that you start with an area in which you are knowledgeable or passionate and then determine how to convey that information in a book. I have a friend who has coached youth sports for much of his adult life. He is also the parent of two boys who love sports. He has written a book for adults on how to coach their kids. Another friend of mine has been a midwife for over 20 years. She wrote a book targeted at expectant mothers. She discussed the benefits of using a midwife and discussed whether expecting parents should use a midwife or a doctor. Both the parent–coach and the midwife conveyed valuable information in their books and they've derived monthly supplementary income from the sales of those books.

In determining a topic for your book or books, don't be discouraged if there are already multiple books available on the subject you're considering. This might be a plus instead of a minus. For example, if you want to write a book on nutrition, you'll quickly note that you'll not be the first person to do so. There are thousands of books out there on nutrition. This should not discourage you, as it shows that there is definitely an interest in the subject. If you can bring a unique perspective to any topic, you'll have a chance to be successful in selling your book.

Develop a Working Title. Jot down ideas for the title of your book as you come up with them. This so-called title will simply be a working title, and you'll be able to change it any time before the book is published. But your working title will serve as a constant reminder of the topic of your book. If you are writing a self-help book, you will certainly want to come up with a title that will entice the reader to buy and read the book. Titles like "How to Lose 10 Pounds in 10 Days" and "How to Train Your New Puppy" will allow prospective buyers and readers to immediately determine if they have further interest in your book.

Develop an Outline. In writing a book, it's going to be important for you to establish some sort of organization with the content of that book. With this in mind, you'll need to develop an outline for the content of that book, possibly even a chapter by chapter outline which you can adhere to in writing the book.

Select a Template for Your Book. Many novice authors find it easier to use a template in writing their books. There are multiple sites on the internet that offer free book templates, including hubspot.com. In some instances, you'll have a number of different templates you can choose from. These templates will help you stay organized throughout the process of writing your book. As you become more accomplished or experienced at writing books, you probably won't need a template. However, it is a valuable tool for beginners.

Write the Book. After you've done all of the above, it's time to get into the nitty-gritty of writing the book itself. This, along with any research which might be required, will probably be the most time-consuming element in making a book. Most experienced authors will set a designated time to write their books, e.g., 2 hours a day, 15 hours a week, etc. They'll also determine which time of the day is best for them to do their writing, e.g., early morning, late evening after the kids have gone to bed, etc.

What if you're not a good writer or what if you have valuable information or a great story to impart to others but don't know how to put it on paper? If this is the case, you're probably going to have to hire someone to write your book for you. Ghostwriters are available on many sites, including Upwork.com. If you're going to hire a freelancer to write your book or your story, I encourage you to remember that they are only going to be able to be as good as the information you provide them with. I've ghostwritten many books and have gathered the information in a number of ways, including a written outline from the person who wants the book written, a collection of blogs by the same person, a weekly one- or two-hour tape-recorded phone interview or Skype interview, etc. Either way, you will have to figure out how to get the necessary information to the freelancer. If you are hiring a freelancer you haven't worked with before, I encourage you to request samples of their writing so you can review the quality and style of their writing and make sure it complies with your expectations. Along the same lines, in working with a freelancer, I suggest that you ask them to write the first chapter of your book for a nominal fee and then proceed with the remainder of the book after you've made sure you're on the right track. This sample chapter will benefit both you and the freelancer, as you'll want to make sure you're "on the same page" before you get too far into the project.

Adding Illustrations, Graphs, Photos. After you've written the book, you should determine whether the addition of illustrations, graphs, or photos will add value to the book. As an example, I just finished writing a book which tells the true story of a former US naval officer who was a Japanese prisoner-of-war in the Philippines in World War II. Although the story itself was incredible, I knew that adding photos to the book would add to the value, as I knew that the readers would want to see the man whose story we told. And even though these were old black-and-white photos and weren't in mint condition, they added value to the book and we opted to include them. A friend of mine recently completed a pie recipe book. Obviously, photos of the pies add a lot to the value of the book, as people who buy recipe books are accustomed to photos of the recipe items. This friend had a limited budget in producing this recipe book, so she opted to take photos of the different pies with her cell phone instead of paying a professional photographer to do so.

Cover Design. Whether you're producing a printed book or an eBook, you should know that how you package that book is likely to be an extremely important factor in the sales of the book. If you've ever browsed books in a bookstore or in the library, you'll know that the cover or jacket of a book can certainly influence whether you buy that book or select that book to read. Packaging is very important. With this in mind, you'll want to create an attractive cover for your book. Unless you are a designer (most of us aren't), you're going to have to hire a freelancer to design your cover. Please know that there are many graphic artists who specialize in designing book covers. I have previously used the fiverr.com site to hire freelancers for my cover designs. I have always been able to hire someone for under $100 to do that and I've been able to get some great designs. Again, with these freelancers, their success may well depend on the instructions you give them. On the Fiverr site, you'll have many freelancers to choose from. In working with them, you have to tell them the size of the book you are looking to produce, whether you want a cover designed for a print book or an eBook or both, and you'll also have to provide the copy that you want on the cover of the book, including the title and a brief description of the book.

In working with freelancers to design covers, I have almost always opted to give them a photo or illustration which I want them to use on the cover. There are a number of stock photo sites on the internet which offer huge selections and excellent search engines for you to find photos or illustrations that you can use on your book covers. I have previously used istockphoto.com for my photo and illustration needs. On this site, I have generally been able to purchase a photograph for under $35 to use on my book covers. These are non-licensed photographs in which the photographers or illustrators post photos or illustrations on the site which are available for purchase on an on-going basis. The photographers or illustrators than get a cut every time a customer purchases their photo or illustration.

Formatting. Whether you want a printed book, an eBook, or both, your book is going to have to be formatted so it can be properly uploaded to the sites that will print or sell your book. If you have the time, you can certainly learn how to do the formatting yourself through tutorials on the internet. If you don't have the time (most people don't), you can always hire a freelancer to do that for you. Again, fiverr.com offers a wide selection of freelancers who will format your book for prices advertised from $15 to $100. In hiring a freelancer to format your book, you'll again need to give them the size of the book if you're going to have a printed book. You're also going to have to tell them who you plan to use to print or sell your books. In working with freelancers on some sites like the Fiverr site, please remember that these freelancers are from all over the world and there may be time differences or language differences involved. With many of these freelancers, English is a second language, but most of them are quite proficient in English. And most of them have done numerous formatting or cover design projects, so they're likely to know exactly what you will need to submit to various self-publishing platforms.

ISBN. If you're going to have a printed book, you'll need an ISBN. ISBN stands for International Standard Book Number and it is a 13-digit number used by publishers, booksellers, and libraries to identify books. ISBN numbers are not required for eBooks. Purchasing an ISBN is a simple process and there are a number of ISBN sellers on the internet. I use isbnservices.com and paid $18.99 for my most recent ISBN. That ISBN includes a barcode which can be used for scanning by booksellers and libraries.

Determining Your Sell Price. As a self-published author, you can set your own selling price. (If you were using a traditional publisher, they would dictate what price you sell at.) In determining a selling price, I always instruct authors to get on publishing platforms such as Amazon to find out what the books in their genre are selling for. Once you have determined that, you should settle on a selling price which falls somewhere within that range. If you are offering a printed version of the book, your sell price should be printed on the back cover of your book inside the ISBN and bar code area. In determining a price for a printed book, please remember that you should select the highest possible price you would sell the book at and then note that you will be able to discount that book when and if you see fit to do so. For example, I wrote a 250-page memoir for which I decided the maximum sell price would be $16. I set this price not only because it was comparable to the prices of other memoirs, but because I wanted my readers who ordered a printed copy from Amazon to be able to spend $20 or less, including shipping. I then made some personal appearances at book clubs and libraries and bookstores, and, in the case of book clubs and libraries, I was able to discount the book to $12 or $14 if they purchased on the spot. This was attractive to prospective readers as everyone likes a discount and they wouldn't have to pay for shipping as they would if they ordered from an internet source. At the time I was doing that (a few years ago), I was paying somewhere between $3 and $4 per book and buying about 25 to 50 books at a time for my presentations, so you can see that my profit margin was still very good, even when I discounted the book.

Pricing for eBooks is slightly different and prices are usually substantially less because there are no actual printing or materials involved. Most eBooks will sell anywhere from $2.99 to $9.99. If you use the Amazon Kindle Direct Publishing (KDP) platform to sell your book, you can expect royalties of 70% on any books that are sold within that $2.99-$9.99 price range. Anything that falls outside that price range, higher or lower, your royalties will drop to 35%. As you can see by those numbers, Amazon strongly prefers that you sell your eBooks on their platform for $2.99-$9.99. And eBooks are different than printed books in that you can't discount them whenever you see fit. For the most part, the selling price you establish is the price you'll sell the book. That said, you should note that KDP offers prospective readers the opportunity to sample a free chapter to see if they want to buy the book. They also offer a giveaway program in which you can offer your book for free when the book is first posted for sale, in an attempt to create interest for the book. Many authors have used this free offer to successfully promote their book and create subsequent sales from the interest they create.

In determining your price for eBooks, the genre of the book will be very important in determining the price. For example, if it is a romance book for which you are hoping for mass consumption, then you'll note that most of these romance novels are sold at the lower end of the price spectrum. On the other hand, if you have a historical non-fiction book such as the book I mentioned concerning the US naval officer who was a Japanese prisoner-of-war, you can probably get more money for that book, as it is a non-fiction account that is not targeted for mass consumption and will appeal mostly to war veterans and history buffs.

Upload Your Book. Now things start to get exciting. You're ready to roll. Your book is finished and it's time to upload it to the platform or platforms on which you intend to sell it. There are many platforms available for you to use in selling your book. I will outline a few of them here for your convenience, but please remember that there are additional options available to you.

1) **Amazon/Kindle.** This is the most well-known platform for selling self-published books. Over two-thirds of all eBook purchases are made through Amazon's Kindle Direct Publishing (KDP), the platform I mentioned in the section immediately preceding this one. If you're serious about selling your book as a passive income stream, Amazon's Kindle platform should be at or near the top of your list. One of the things that make the KDP platform so popular is that your prospective readers can get the Kindle app for their computer, tablet, or phone. This means that it will be easy for them to purchase and read your book. Amazon also has a partnership with Audible which will allow you to easily convert your book to an audio format and sell additional books. I'll go into further detail on audiobooks in the paragraphs that follow. So, one of the big advantages of using the Amazon platform to sell your book is that it is the most popular platform for buying and selling books. Also, it offers you the opportunity to publish digital, printed, and audio versions of your book all in one platform.
2) **Nook.** Barnes & Noble is a large book retailer and their e-reader device is called the Nook. The Nook is responsible for about a quarter of all e-readership so this is another platform that you should strongly consider for any book you want to sell. Royalties with the Nook platform are very similar to those of Amazon/Kindle. Nook royalties are 65% of the list price for any books sold between $2.99 and $9.99; 40% for books sold outside that range.
3) **iBooks.** Publishing your book on iBooks will allow you to sell your books in the Apple iBookstore. It means that your book can be made available to anyone that has an iPhone, and IPad, or a Mac, all Apple devices.

4) **Others.** I've outlined the three main platforms above, but you should know that there are also other platforms available for you to use in selling your book. Although I won't go into detail with those other options here, I would at least like to mention a few of them, so you can research yourself if you have further interest. Platforms such as Smashwords, Kobo, and Scribd are also very viable platforms on which to sell books. They might not offer the large numbers that the "big three" platforms do, but they still offer the opportunity for you to sell more books and make more money.

Marketing Your Book. Tips for Maximizing Your Book Profits

Marketing Your Book. Just because you've finished writing your book and posted it for sale on various platforms doesn't mean that you're done. Marketing your book is one of the most crucial factors in making money from your book. A number of years ago, a friend of mine hosted a New Year's Eve party for his friends and co-workers. He purchased large amounts of food and cold beverages for his party, presuming that it would be the party of the year. When the clock struck midnight and the new year rolled in, he asked me what I thought was the reason why only less than a dozen people at his party. "I'm not sure", I responded. "Did you tell people you were having the party?" My friend responded that he had been so busy making party plans that he hadn't had the chance to tell a lot of people about the party. As he himself said, "I thought the word would get around."

Well, the same goes for your book. Now that you've invested time and money to write your book, it's time to tell people that it's available. You can't expect people to buy your book if they don't even know it exists.

With this in mind, I have some tips for you to market your book and sell it. If you want to maximize the extra money you earn from your book, you'll need to market it. And if you can market it successfully, you might be able to reap financial benefits from it for quite some time.

Here are some simple and inexpensive ways you can market your book:

1) **Social Media.** Most of us already have a social media presence. Social media offers you a great opportunity to get the word out about your new book. Authors have used social media platforms such as Facebook, Instagram, Twitter, Tumblr, Reddit, and Pinterest to promote their new books. In many instances, they would offer a free sample for readers in an effort to get them interested to buy the book. Also, please know that you should not just use these platforms once to promote your book. I've used those platforms multiple times, to announce that the book is available, to publish positive reviews I get on the book, to remind people that your book would make a great holiday gift, etc.

2) **Blogs, Websites.** Do you have a blog or a website which you can use to direct visitors to the platforms where they can purchase your book? If so, you should make sure you use these platforms to promote your book. If not, you may want to consider creating a blog to promote your new book and any future books.

3) **Emails, Texts.** I have also used mass emails and texts to announce the availability of my books. Over the years, I've accumulated a substantial address book. All of these people are potential customers. So, whenever I have a new book available, I send a mass email to my contacts,

including a sales flyer which shows the cover of the book along with a brief description of the book and where they can purchase the book.

4) **Bookmarks, Postcards.** Also, each time I have a new book out, I print some bookmarks and postcards which I can hand out to people that I meet in person. I don't actually mail many of the postcards, but I like to hand them out to people I meet. I like the size of postcards because they can contain more information than the smaller bookmarks. Bookmarks and postcards are inexpensive ways to promote your book. I think I paid $25 plus shipping for 500 bookmarks and $30 plus shipping for 500 postcards from an online source. I use these items almost like business cards, handing them out readily to just about everyone I meet.

Tips for Publishing Audio Books

The audiobook market is yet another platform for you to use in enhancing your self-published book sales. Although the audiobook market isn't as large as the printed book or eBook market, it is a burgeoning market that merits your consideration. In a day and age where podcasts and radio apps are popular, it is important to note that some people prefer to view or listen to things instead of reading them. Whether they are driving in a car, working out at the health club, or lying on the beach, some people like to listen to audiobooks. And, of course, there are other people who just don't like to read and they prefer audio or visual methods.

I'm of the belief that you should wait to see how successful your printed books or eBooks are before you decide to publish them as audiobooks. The reason I say this is because of the extra time and extra expense involved. Before you invest more time or money in your book, you should first determine if it is successful in printed or eBook format. If so, you should definitely publish your book in audio format. If you don't, you'll be leaving money on the table that you could be earning by using an audio format.

Audiobook Creation Exchange (ACX) is the most popular platform for audiobooks. If you add your audiobook to ACX, it will be available for sale on Amazon, Audible, and the Apple Audio Store. For those of you not familiar with Audible, it is a seller and producer of spoken audio entertainment, information, and educational programming on the internet. It is a top seller of digital audiobooks.

If you publish your book on ACX, you'll earn royalties of 20% to 40% of whatever your sell price is.

Here is some quick general information regarding converting your book from a printed or digital format to an audio format.

1) **Prepare Your Book for Audio.** You'll need to edit your printed or digital books so they can be used as audiobooks. In other words, remove everything that won't make sense in an audio format, i.e., no references to illustrations, photos, or graphs; no hyperlinks or "click here" prompts.

2) **Decide Who Will Record Your Audio.** If you're going to have an audiobook, you're going to have to determine who will record your book? Will you want to hire a narrator or will you want to record the book in your own voice? If you have an education book or a memoir, you'll be more likely to be the narrator for your own book than you would for a book of fiction in which you may be better served to use someone with an acting skillset. In my own experience, I have always hired a narrator, even for my own memoir. I've done that for a number of reasons, but mostly because I don't have a great narrator's voice. My throat gets dry very quickly when I talk a

lot, and I'm sure that it would take me long periods of time to narrate a book so listeners would quickly tire of my raspy voice. Also, I have a relatively noisy home environment, including a lot of street noise, and I am afraid the background noise would be too distracting to the listener. I had thought previously about renting a recording studio to record my book, but I feel that the money I would have spent renting a studio could just as well be spent in paying a narrator.

3) **Hiring a Narrator.** Hiring a narrator may not be as expensive as you might think. I have an associate who hires narrators on a frequent basis and he is usually able to hire someone for less than $500. He tells me that there are two sites he would recommend in hiring a freelance narrator. Those sites are Upwork and Voices. ACX also has narrators you can hire for your book. In hiring any freelance narrator, you should absolutely ask them to provide previous samples of their work. And, you might also ask them to narrate a small portion of your book before you officially hire them. In this way, you can make sure they are a good fit for your project before you get too far into the book.

4) **Rent a Recording Studio; Narrate Your Own Book.** If you want to narrate your own book, and if your home or office environment is too noisy to do so, you may have to rent a recording studio to use in narrating your book. I have a friend who tells me that this can be a 10- to 20-hour process, depending on the length of your book, so you may have to book the studio for multiple days. Again, beware that using your voice for such a long period of time may affect the quality of your voice, so you might have to rent the studio in smaller blocks of maybe three or four hours at a time.

If you want to learn more about creating an audiobook, I suggest that you visit selfpublishingschool.com, where Chandler Bolt has an extensive article on exactly how to publish an audiobook.

Six Steps Toward Earning Extra Income by Publishing Online Courses

I'd be remiss if I did not discuss how publishing online courses can create additional revenue streams for you. The market for online courses and online learning is getting bigger and bigger. The research firm Global Market Insights projects that online learning courses could reach $240 billion by 2023. That's an astronomical number.

With this in mind, I encourage you to consider developing online courses to create additional passive income streams for yourself. Here are some simple tips to get you started on developing an online course or courses:

1) **Find a topic.** What are you an expert at? Do you have information that is valuable to others...to the point that others will be willing to pay to learn that information? Or, even if you are not an expert, can you become an expert? One of the major success stories in online courses is that of Purna Duggirala, a man from India who goes by the name of Chandoo. A number of years ago, Chandoo recognized an opportunity to make money by hosting online courses. He noticed that people did not properly know how to use the Excel software program, so he came up with a series of courses in which he taught subscribers how to become excellent or awesome at Excel. He made over $1 million in 2014 with that concept. Again, we all know that these success stories only show the top range a person can earn. It's unlikely that you'll earn that kind of cash with your online

courses. But again, there's no harm in dreaming. Even if you can garner an additional $500 to $1000 every month from your online course or courses, I'm sure you'd take it.

In determining a topic for your online courses, I suggest that you first take a personal inventory of your own knowledge to see if there is anything you can impart to people who would be willing to pay for your expertise. Are you an expert at technology? Can you teach coding or programming? Do you speak multiple languages? Can you teach one of those languages to people who are planning to visit a foreign country? A friend of mine is originally from the Philippines. Besides now speaking impeccable English, she speaks fluent Visayan and Tagalog, two languages that are spoken by many Filipinos. So, with the ability to speak these languages, she created an online mini-course series in which she teaches English-speaking people who are getting ready to visit the Philippines how to speak those native languages. She has been quite successful in getting people to subscribe to her courses and has derived a nice supplemental income from those courses.

If you don't have any areas where you would consider yourself an expert, you can always become an expert simply by garnering the information you have a passion for and then inserting that information into a course that is available online to others. I read a story about a man who knew nothing about coding, but by the time he finished reading multiple books on the subject, taking some online courses and tutorials, he knew more than almost all of the people who were interested in the same subject. So even though he hadn't started out as an expert, he became an expert with valuable information that people were willing to pay for.

2) **Create a course outline.** If you're going to create an online course, you'll most certainly need an outline for that course. You'll not only use that outline in conveying information to subscribers, but you'll also use that outline to sell the course to prospective subscribers, who are sure to want to know what the course entails before they enroll in it. In setting up your course, please know that most online courses are limited to a maximum of 20 minutes per session. After that, subscribers start to lose interest. I strongly suggest that you set up a series of 15- to 20-minute courses that can teach people everything they want to know about whatever subject you're teaching. That might entail as few as three-course sessions or as many as 10. Either way, limit your sessions to 20 minutes. And remember, each course should get your subscribers closer to the goals and objectives of your course.

3) **Determine the price of your course.** In determining a price for your online course, please know that the length of the course should not be the main determinant. First, you should check to see what your competitors in the same subject are selling their courses for. Then, you should look at how your expertise falls within the spectrum of those people who are offering similar courses. For example, if Bill Gates or Paul Allen were to offer a course on how to use Windows, it's safe to assume that you're probably not going to be able to charge the same amount for a similar course. I say that somewhat tongue-in-cheek, but if you're a neophyte in the field for which your offering an online course, you're probably not going to be able to charge as much as an expert in the field. Finally, in determining the price for your online course, you should consider how much value you are giving the course subscriber. For example, if you're going to offer

an online course which can be used to make thousands of dollars, you should be able to charge a lot more for that course than you would in offering to teach Portuguese to people who are planning on visiting Brazil. Or if your online course is solving a problem, a course that solves a major problem should obviously be priced higher than a course that solves a minor problem. Use common sense to set your sell price, and don't be afraid to test different price points. It's your course and you should be able to set whatever price you like for that course, as long as people are willing to subscribe.

I'd like to mention one other thing in regards to pricing for online courses. Yes, you'll be able to make money if you can <u>tell</u> people how to do something, but you'll be able to make even more money if you can <u>show</u> them how to do something. And finally, you'll be able to charge even more if you can offer support for the information you are trying to teach. For example, if you have a course on how to self-publish a book, are you available to answer individual questions your subscribers might have.

4) **Create the course content.** Using your course outline, you should create course content for each of your lesson segments. Depending on your own personal preference, you can decide whether you'll want to work from a script or not, but you'll definitely want to work from an outline. Many of the most successful online courses do not work from a script and are more casual and conversational, but almost all of them work from an outline.

5) **Create the course.** Your next step is to create the course itself. By now, you'll have decided if your course is going to be a written course, an audio course, or a video course.

Obviously, video courses are the most successful, because people like to see visuals as they learn. If you're going to do a video course, you won't need to hire a video expert to shoot or edit your lessons. You should be able to do this on your phone, and you should know that there are many easy-to-use tools and software programs available. Programs such as Camtasia and Quicktime are among the programs that can be used for screen recordings.

When you are creating your course, you should remind yourself that it's not realistic to expect your lesson video recording to have the feel of a major television production. The content of the lesson will be more important than the presentation and you will certainly get better at the production of your lessons as you become more experienced at doing so.

6) **Launch your course.** There are a ton of different platforms available to host your online courses. Instead of trying to go through a multitude of these platforms, I will tell you how one of the most popular platforms works so you can get an idea of what you might expect in publishing and selling the online courses you develop. Udemy.com is the world's largest online learning platform. More than 30 million students have taken courses on Udemy; over 50,000 instructors offer over 130,000 courses in over 60 languages. This will give you an idea of the scope of the Udemy platform. Anyone can post a course on Udemy. If you want to charge a fee to the students on Udemy, you will need to complete a free application which is usually approved within two days. For any students you get to take your course, you will receive 97% of the course fee. Udemy will take a 3% commission. If Udemy secures students for your courses via

their own marketing, they will then take a 50% commission amount and the instructor will receive the other 50%. As Udemy does not charge a hosting fee, the only way they make money is by selling courses. Udemy is widely known as a good place to start for the novice online instructors, as it offers a simple way for instructors/sellers to assemble content like PowerPoint slides, PDF documents, and YouTube videos into a coherent course. The Udemy platform also offers a variety of marketing tools to help sellers sell their course.

Other popular online learning course platforms include Teachable, WizIQ, Thinkific, and Ruzuka. If you want to take a more in-depth look at the different online course platforms which are available, I recommend that you visit www.learningrevolution.net/sell-online-courses/, where they have a nice article outlining 15 of the best online learning course platforms.

Whether you're publishing printed books, digital books, audiobooks, or online learning courses, these self-publishing methods offer you some excellent opportunities to create passive income streams which can make you money for long periods of time after you've done the initial work to develop the materials. These self-publishing venues are not 100% passive income, as there is some initial work required. However, once you have published the materials, you should be able to derive additional income for long periods of time—weeks, months, even years—with very little additional work.

Chapter 3--Blogging for Big Profits

Another great way for you to create additional passive income will be for you to create a series of blogs. We're all familiar with the multitude of blogs that appear on the internet, but you may not understand exactly how bloggers make income from their blogs. With this chapter, I will provide some tips on how you can start a successful blog that can provide you with additional income. Like most passive income streams, starting a blog will require some time and effort. But once you are set up, your blogs can continue to provide income for months, weeks, and even years.

The Truth About Earning Through Blogs

I'm sure you're aware that there are millions of blogs on the internet. Anyone who has used Google or Bing can attest to the fact that there is a blog on the internet for just about every topic imaginable. Some of those blogs make money; some of them don't. Some of those blogs are intended to make money; others are not. Some of the blogs intended to make money do not make money. With this chapter, we will concentrate on blogs that are intended to make money and I will give you some tips and techniques as to how to create a blog and then how to monetize that blog.

Determine a Niche. In starting a blog that is going to provide you with additional income, you will first have to find a niche for that blog. A niche is a particular market segment or audience. Unless your blog has a specific niche or target audience, it's going to be very difficult for you to monetize it. Yes, there are bloggers on the internet who write about random topics or about anything and everything. But most of those bloggers don't make money from their blogs. Bloggers who make money from their blogs usually have specific topics or niches that they use to attract visitors to their site or solve specific problems.

In determining a niche for your blog, you should remember that most people visit blogs to gather information or to solve a specific problem. If you can provide them with the information they are looking for in an attractive package, then you'll have a chance to have a successful blog. It's important to note that whatever niche you choose, there are probably already existing blogs that already fall within that niche. Don't let this discourage you. If you can convey valuable information and you can convey it in a straightforward, entertaining, and attractive manner, you'll have a chance to be successful with your blog.

Here are examples of some of the most popular blog niches:

    --How to Make Money.

    --Health & Fitness.

    --Lifestyle.

    --Food.

    --Personal Finance.

    --Beauty and Fashion.

In choosing a niche for your blog, I strongly suggest that you select a topic or an area that you are passionate about. If you are passionate about something, you'll be much more likely to be able to write blogs about that subject. Your readers will be able to sense your passion and you'll be a lot less likely to abandon your blog or blog series because you've become bored with it or lost interest in it.

I'll give you an example. I have a close friend who is an avid baseball fan. His favorite team is the Minnesota Twins professional baseball team. My friend, who when I first met him was working a regular day job, is such a baseball fan that he spends almost all of his spare time thinking and talking about baseball. He lives and breathes baseball. One day, it dawned on him that he might be able to make money from his favorite hobby. So, he started a Minnesota Twins baseball blog in which he posted articles he wrote about his favorite team. He found quickly that there were many other Minnesota Twins fans who were desperate to read about their team every day and they wanted a daily dose of information about the Twins, even during the off-season. So, what started as a weekly blog, quickly became a daily blog or post. He now has a stable of regular contributors who contribute to his Minnesota Twins-themed website. He has a forum in which his site visitors or blog readers can comment on various subjects involving the Twins. The site now has semi-monthly podcasts in which he and some of his associates discuss the Twins. He is a guest on radio shows and talks about the Twins. Bottom line, he has turned his passion and his modest initial blogs into a full-time job. He is truly doing what he loves. His Twins website/blog spot now gets so many daily visitors that he is easily able to sell site advertising to companies that are looking to reach the same niche audience. Those advertisers include ticket brokers, bars and restaurants that are near the Twins stadium, travel agencies that coordinate spring training vacations to watch the Twins, etc. It's amazing to think that all of this started with one paltry blog and has blossomed into a full-scale profitable business.

In reviewing this example, it is important to remember that my friend selected a niche he was passionate about, one he was not going to lose interest in. He was going to think and talk baseball whether he had a blog or not. But in launching his blog, he quickly discovered that many people have the same passion he has, and he was able to monetize that passion into a profitable business.

If you want to determine a possible niche for your blog and you're not quite sure what a good niche would be for you, let me suggest that you ask yourself the following questions: What is your favorite hobby? How do you spend most of your free time? Is there a subject or topic that you could go on and on about if someone is willing to listen? What were your favorite subjects in high school or college? What things do you like to read about, learn about, or gather information on?   If you were independently wealthy and you did not have to work for a living, what activities or pastimes would you choose to fill your time?

Write Some Blogs. Once you have determined your niche, you can start writing blogs. Instead of writing just one blog, I suggest that you write a series of blogs so you can post them on a regular basis (weekly, monthly, etc.). Prepare some kind of an outline in which you determine and detail the topics for each of your blogs. Some bloggers prefer to place all their content online at the same time and then leave it at that. For example, if the niche is targeted at bloggers and is How to Start and Make Money from a Blog, the blogger could post a number of blogs all at the same time. Topics for the individual blogs could include how to choose a blog niche, how to write a blog, how to choose a blog platform, ways to make money from your blog, etc. Each different topic could have a separate blog and, in reality, you could post all of these blogs at the same time and be done with the writing. On the other hand, if your niche requires or benefits from frequent updating, you'll want to write additional blogs as new information becomes available. For example, with the Minnesota Twins blog site I described, the Twins play 162 games in a regular season and it's reasonable to think that any blogs concerning the team will require at least weekly blogs. This particular site has become so successful that it now features new blogs on a daily basis. It's important to note that these blogs are not all written by the founder of the blog site. He now has a stable of writers who contribute blogs to the site on a regular basis.

What if you're not a writer? Can you still have a blog? Yes, you can. You can hire a freelancer to write your blogs. There are a number of freelancing sites you can use to hire a writer, including Upwork and Fiverr. If you want to convey specific information in your blogs, then you will obviously have to relay this information to the freelance writer. But I know other people who simply give the freelancer a topic and then the freelancer will research the topic and write the article. In hiring a freelancer, you should try to find someone that fits your style and someone you can work with on an on-going basis. You may have to go through a freelancer or two before you can find a freelancer that suits your needs. Depending on the length of your blogs, you should be able to find a freelancer that can write a blog for you at about $25 to $40 per blog. If research is required on the part of the freelancer, you can expect to pay more.

Select Your Platform. There are a lot of different platforms available for you to publish your blog. Some of them are free; others charge a nominal monthly fee to host your blogs. In this section, I'll detail a few of the options available to you and then you can research these options further as you decide which platform you should use.

> 1) **WordPress** is the most popular blogging platform. It is especially popular with beginner bloggers as it is free, it doesn't require a lot of technical expertise such as coding or design, and it has lots of different themes to choose from. Please know that WordPress might not have the functionality you are looking for unless you pay for their upgrades. However, as a beginner, you can decide which

"bells and whistles" you want to upgrade to later to make your site look more professional, to have access to more themes, designs, and plug-ins, etc. For example, WordPress.org charges about $3 a month for hosting and offers more than 1500 free themes and 20,000 free plug-in options. Again, if you are a beginner, I suggest that you start with the free package and see if that fits your needs. If not, you will be able to upgrade at any time.

2) **Blogger** is a platform owned by Google. It's also free and offers free access to Google tools such as AdSense and Analytics. It is an easy platform to use and it's a great platform for beginner bloggers.

3) **Tumblr** is another free platform that is a social media site. It's great for microbloggers, people who want to post many short notes frequently.

4) **Typepad** and **WIX** are pay-per-month business platforms that charge nominal monthly hosting fees of less than $10 per month. Those platforms are geared toward business blogs. They are easy to use. WIX has ecommerce functions that make it attractive to small businesses. Unlike WordPress, Blogger, and Tumblr, both Typepad and Wix allow you to have your own domain name. For example, your domain name will always have wordpress (Wordpress) or blogspot (Blogger) in the title. This may not matter to you, but if you are a business, that might be an important consideration and you may want instead use a third party server such as BlueHost or HostGator to host your site. Both of those third-party servers offer very reasonable pricing for hosting at less than $3 a month.

Promote Your Blog. Common sense tells us that no one is going to read your blog unless they know it exists. Some bloggers are reluctant to "toot their own horn" and tell others that they have a blog. Don't be shy about this. When you publish your first blog, use email blasts and social media to tell people you know about your new blog and tell them how they can access it. If you don't do this, then you may find that your mother is the only person reading it.

Use Your Blog to Expand Other Related Passive Income Activities. If you're smart, you will tie your blogs into your other passive income activities. Not only will this help produce additional income, it should also help you create a loyal following. Many people use their blogs to promote their newsletters. They will instruct readers to sign up for monthly or quarterly newsletters. Along the same lines, bloggers will direct their readers to the podcasts or the videos they have produced. I know quite a number of bloggers who have accumulated the blogs they've written over the years and compiled those blogs into eBooks. It's all interrelated. You should plan to have multiple venues to promote your passive income activities.

Seven Ways to Earn Income from Blogging

There are multiple ways you can make money from blogging. No, it's not an overnight process and there is some initial work required. However, once you're up and running, you could be able to supplement your income substantially by blogging. I've selected seven of my favorite ways for you to make money blogging. Here they are:

1) **Cost-per-click (CPC) advertising.** With this concept, advertisers will pay each time a visitor to your site clicks on one of the ads on your site. It's a "finder's fee" of sorts. CPC advertising can include full-color ads which appear on your site; it can also include simple text advertising in your blog.

For example, if you have a baseball blog in which the topic is "Different ways to get tickets to the big game" and one of the options is to buy tickets from an authorized ticket broker, you would be able to mention the name of that ticket broker in your text, and, provided that the ticket broker is a participating advertiser, you'll be able to earn a small sum every time someone clicks on that ad and the ad takes them to the advertiser's site. I should mention up front that you're not going to get rich from CPC advertising until the numbers of people visiting your site reach respectable numbers. Companies that offer easy to implement CPC internet advertising include Google's AdSense, infolinks, media.net, and Chitika. If you have further interest in CPC advertising, I suggest that you visit some of these aforementioned sites to learn more about what advertising programs are available to you as a blogger.

2) **Sell your own advertising on your blog.** If you want, you can take it upon yourself to go "old school" and sell ads on your site. You can arrange yourself for advertisers on your site or you can have a third-party seller do that for you. To give you an example of a sell-your-own advertising approach, if you have a blog regarding a specific bike trail, you could certainly approach a bike rental place along that trail or a restaurant at one of the stops along the trail and see if they want to advertise on your blog. Nothing wrong with selling ads to your blog the old-fashioned way…and you will be able to keep 100% of the ad revenue yourself. If you don't want to bother with selling ads on your site, you can register with a third-party seller and they can do that for you. Companies like BuySellAds or BlogAds are third-party advertising sellers who will sell ads for your blog. They'll then give you 70 to 75% of the ad sales and then keep the remaining amounts in

return for their efforts. Please note that third-party sellers are not interested in low-traffic blogs, so you'll have to get your traffic to a decent level before you can even consider using a third-party seller.

3) **Sell text links on your blog.** I mentioned text link advertising in the above section on CPC advertising. There is a company called LinkWorth that specializes in this kind of text advertising. With LinkWorth, you'll be able to link a piece of text in your blog to a page on another site. Every time one of your blog readers clicks on this link, you'll receive a commission from Linkworth. This is another program that requires a decent amount of traffic to your blog before you can begin working with LinkWorth, so if you're a new blogger and your blog traffic is still minimal, you'll have to get your traffic up before you can begin doing these cost-per-click text links.

4) **Online courses and workshops.** In the previous chapter, I told you how you could make money by self-publishing online courses and workshops. Any blog you do should link to any related online courses and workshops that you've produced. Again, all of these things are interrelated and you should never miss an opportunity to advertise one medium on another medium.

5) **Books and eBooks.** Just as you'll want to use your blog to promote your online courses and workshops, you'll want to use it to promote any printed books, digital books, or audiobooks which you have produced.

6) **Speaking gigs.** Once your blog traffic has reached a reputable level, you will be able to advertise yourself as an expert on whatever subject your blog covers. This may bring speaking opportunities in which you can enhance your passive income. I had a recent speaking engagement which resulted

from my blogs concerning the history of the small town I was born in. My audience was the town historical society and, although I didn't get paid for my speaking engagement, I was able to sell 71 of my printed books after my presentation. The presentation was well worth my time financially, as I made over $10 per printed book for a 90-minute presentation which I enjoyed immensely. So, if you're not yet someone who can command a fee of $10,000 to $100,000 per speech, don't worry about it. You can still achieve profits on a lower scale by using your blog to promote your products and services.

7) **Affiliate marketing.** Affiliate marketing involves recommending or referring the products and services of other companies and their products and services in return for a commission. Are you recommending other products or services on your blog? Or could you recommend other products or services on your blog? If you do or if you can, then I suggest that you consider affiliate marketing to earn some passive income. Again, the money you can earn will be directly related to the number of people who read your blogs, however when your blog traffic reaches a respectable level, then it's time for you to start exploring affiliate marketing opportunities. There are a ton of affiliate programs available to you. I've listed some of the most popular programs for you to use as a starting point when your blog is at a level where you can start to reap the benefits of affiliate marketing. (I've provided additional information about affiliate marketing in the chapter that follows.)

--Amazon Associates

--eBay Partner Network

--BlueHost

--HostGator

--HostPapa

--DreamHost

--AliExpress

As I've detailed in this chapter, you will be able to earn passive income from your blog. Obviously, before you can do that, you'll have to get your blog up and running and get the traffic levels for that blog to a point where you can earn some extra cash from it. But once you've done that, you can start reaping the benefits from it.

Chapter 4—Make Passive Income on the Internet Now

Most of us have heard the term "make money while you are sleeping". Affiliate marketing is the passive income activity which is most often associated with the concept of making money while you are sleeping. In this chapter, I'll outline how you can make money with affiliate marketing and with dropshipping, another passive income activity which is often related to affiliate marketing. I'll tell you why you need to consider these activities for your passive income streams and I'll tell you how to get started.

All You Need to Know About Affiliate Marketing

Affiliate marketing is when you recommend or refer the products or services of other companies in return for a commission. With affiliate marketing, you are the affiliate. You search for products that you enjoy or would like to endorse and then promote that product through your various media, including websites, social media, written blogs or video blogs, and emails, and then you earn a portion of the profit when a sale is made for that product or service. Sales are tracked through affiliate links from one website to another.

I'll give you a quick example. A woman has a series of blogs or podcasts that are targeted at new parents. As a new parent herself, she has used a baby stroller which she really likes and would recommend to anyone. With these in mind, she writes one of her blogs or does one of her vlogs (video blogs) with this stroller brand as the main subject. She highly recommends the stroller based on her experience in using it and in her blog or vlog she provides a link to the site of the manufacturer, where customers can visit and subsequently purchase the stroller. For each stroller sold as a result of the woman's blog or vlog, the woman will receive a commission for her part in recommending the stroller and then telling the customer where they can purchase it.

As this book is being written, current statistics show that 81% of all brands and 84% of all companies are using affiliate marketing as a means to sell their products or services. Those percentages will continue to increase as companies continue to increase their affiliate marketing spending. In 2018, 16% of all internet sales resulted from affiliate marketing. That's an impressive number. Data now shows that companies selling products and services through affiliate marketing will spend 62% of what they would spend through traditional marketing efforts, so as these companies realize that they can spend less and be more successful in selling through affiliate marketing, they will begin to focus more of their sales efforts on that activity and affiliate marketing will continue to grow in future years.

From the consumer standpoint, consumers may or may not be aware that you will be earning a commission as a result of recommending a product or service. Either way, most of them won't care, as they will almost always end up paying the same price for the product. Your commission will be built into the retail price of the product and the consumer will not pay additional to cover your commissions.

As an affiliate, you can be paid for three different actions which direct the consumer to the seller. The most popular action will be Pay Per Sales. With this action, you direct the consumer to the seller and the consumer purchases the product. You can also get paid with a Pay for Lead action. Again, you direct the consumer to a seller site and the consumer then does any of a number of required actions, possibly completing a contact form, signing up for a product trial, subscribing to a newsletter, downloading software, etc. In these instances, the seller will value these actions enough to pay you a commission. Another form of affiliate marketing involves the affiliate being paid on a Pay Per Click basis. Usually, Pay Per Click involves the consumer clicking a link on your site to move to the seller's site. The seller values this enough to allocate a commission to the affiliate.

Why be an affiliate marketer? With affiliate marketing, you really can earn money while you are sleeping. Once you've invested an initial amount of time in promoting a product, you can continue to earn money for your efforts long after you recommended the seller's product or service. Once you have directed the consumer to the seller, you can step out of the transaction and don't have to spend any time in supporting the customer after the sale. Affiliate marketing is attractive to many people because it allows them to earn passive income from home without much initial investment and without having to create the product or service you're going to help sell. There are no affiliate fees to worry about and you can get started quickly without a lot of time or effort.

Five Steps Toward Becoming an Affiliate Marketer

How can you get started on your journey to becoming an affiliate marketer? Here are some simple steps you can take to become an affiliate marketer. By the time you complete these steps, you should be well on the road to becoming a successful affiliate marketer and earning passive income while you sleep.

1) **Find or determine a niche.** If you're going to get into affiliate marketing, you're going to have to determine a niche for that marketing. In determining a niche or niches for your affiliate

marketing, I strongly suggest that you find niches or areas that you are passionate about or strongly interested in.

I'll use myself and my wife as examples. In doing a personal inventory, I have a number of passions, many of which are my hobbies. I love baseball, especially Major League Baseball. I also love being a youth baseball coach. I also love reading and writing. I consider myself to be an expert on writing, ghostwriting, self-publishing, and editing. Finally, I love biking and I love dogs. My wife, on the other hand, loves to talk about parenting issues. She is a midwife by trade and is very knowledgeable about midwifery. She is a fashionista and is extremely knowledgeable and passionate about handbags, as our credit card statements attest.

In looking at your interests, you should now try to determine whether there is enough depth there for you to present yourself as an expert on the subject. Is there enough depth in the subject that you could write 25, 50, or 100 blogs about it? For my purposes, I could write a blog about baseball every day. On the other hand, even though I enjoy biking, I would find it difficult to write 25 to 50 blogs about biking.

If you have enough depth in the niche you are considering, the next thing to consider is whether you can make money in recommending products or services in that niche. With the interests of my wife and I, a couple of things pop out at me. Regarding my love for dogs, I am well aware that pet products and supplies are a huge industry. Even a smaller industry such as bicycling has a lot of different products available, including bikes, helmets, gloves, bike bags, water bottles, and bottle holders, bike tire repair kits, etc. Obviously, there is a market for women's handbags, thanks to my wife. On the other hand, it's my feeling that there isn't as much money to be made in the youth coaching, as there aren't many products required to coach a youth baseball team. Yes, uniforms, bats, and balls may be required, but most coaches already have sources for those products. Yes, there may be some online coaching workshops which may be available to sell or some books along the same lines, but the amount of products in this niche seems to be somewhat limited compared to the products available in the dog niche or even in the smaller biking niche. So, in taking an inventory of the things you're passionate about, you should determine if there is money to be made within those niches. If there aren't any or that many products to sell within that niche, then it's not a good affiliate marketing niche. No products mean no sales.

2) **Are there affiliate marketing programs available within your niche?** After you've settled on a niche that you're interested in, it's time for you to find out what's out there in terms of product and services you can promote with your websites, blogs, vlogs, and emails. For example, if I decide that I want to get into an affiliate marketing program regarding puppy training, I'd want to find out what products are out there that are related to puppy training or dog training. On a slightly broader scale, what products are out there that are related to puppies in general.

You'll have to spend some time researching this. But because the products and services you find will be the source of your income for this affiliate marketing endeavor, the time you spend will be well worth it. When you find these products or services, you should make sure they are of good quality. If you are marketing items of poor quality, it will surely damage your reputation or credibility. Many affiliate marketers will test products or services before recommending them. Also, you should make sure that the products you're recommending to consumers are products that you want to be associated with. It might behoove you to read the posted product reviews of any products or services you are considering for your affiliate marketing efforts.

As you find affiliate marketing programs within your niche, you should see if there are similar sellers to you within the niche. If so, that's probably a good indication, as other affiliates would probably not be recommending those sellers if they are not making money from it.

3) **Time to build a site.** Now that you've done your research, it's time for you to create a vehicle in which you can disseminate information to consumers. It's time to build a website. Although there are many different web hosts out there, many beginners use WordPress because it is easy to use and it's free (although upgrades are available). Building a website is much, much easier than ever before and you won't need to be a coder or a designer. No technical knowledge required.

In building a website, you have to first purchase a domain, which will be the address for your website. GoDaddy and NameCheap are both very popular sources from which you can purchase a domain name. The last time I looked, you could purchase domain names from both these companies at under $15 per year. In selecting your domain name, you should know that it's possible that the domain name you want is already in existence and you may have to come up with some other options.

After you have a domain name, you will have to find a host for your website. Again, GoDaddy is a popular option, as are BlueHost and HostGator, companies I previously mentioned.

All three of those companies have plans that start under $3 a month. If you purchase your domain name and your web hosting from different companies, you will need to link the two together. However, this is a very easy process that is outlined on the abovementioned sites.

Now that you have purchased a domain name and selected a host for your website, it's time for you to install your content management system. (e.g., WordPress or whatever content management system you have chosen.) In the process of doing this, you'll have the chance to select a theme to use for your website. While most content management systems offer a large selection of themes to choose from, you should select a theme that works well with whatever niche you have chosen.

4) **Create content for your website.** Now that you have your domain name, your web host, and your theme, you can begin creating content for your website. Whatever content you create should certainly be related to the niche you have chosen. Your content should be interesting enough, engaging enough, or informative enough to keep your web visitors coming back. Here are some basic ideas on popular ways to convey content on affiliate marketing sites:

> **Reviews.** Many affiliates will provide reviews of the products or services they are trying to sell. If possible, you will have used the products you're reviewing. This should help you immensely in reviewing the product. If you haven't used the product, many consumers may be able to sense that you haven't done so.
>
> **Blogs.** Affiliates often use blogs to promote the items they are trying to sell. Although the blog doesn't

necessarily need to be all about the item you're trying to sell, it should at least mention that product or service within the article in the appropriate place. Many blogs will address problems, questions, and then hopefully provide solutions or recommendations on how those problems can be solved. In working your affiliate marketing, you'll obviously want to recommend your affiliate products as possible solutions to the problems.

In-text Content Links. I'm sure you've visited websites and read articles which have links within the text of those articles. If you click on those links, they'll take you to other websites where you can view additional content or purchase products or services. These are called in-text context links and they provide a very effective means of affiliate marketing. By using in-text links, you'll be able to earn money if people from your site go immediately to these other sites and purchase products.

Informational Products. Many websites will offer free informational products to build their mailing lists. If you can build a substantial mailing list, you will be much more successful in your affiliate marketing. Affiliates will also offer free newsletters or free eBooks to consumers who register their names and email addresses.

Banner ads. Many affiliates use banner ads on their websites to direct people to their affiliate sites. These banner ads can be very effective, though you wouldn't want to clutter your site with so many ads that your content gets lost. You might also lose your credibility as an expert.

5) **Market your site, build your audience.** Now that you have your website up and running, it's important to let people know it exists. There are a number of ways you can build the audience for your website. In doing this, it is important for you to continue adding valuable content to your site, content that will keep people coming back to your site. If someone is going to visit your site once and then never visit again, you're very unlikely to be successful in your affiliate marketing efforts. Here are ways you can build your following:

> **Social media.** You're probably already participating in various social media venues. It's important for you to use those venues to promote your new website. Social media such as Facebook, Instagram, Twitter, and Pinterest offer opportunities for you to get the word out about your new site.
>
> **Expertise.** If you are an expert in something (i.e.— puppy training), you should make yourself available to do guest posts on other related high-traffic blogs. Offer to write blogs to be posted on these other sites in return for them mentioning or providing a link to your web address. Guest posting on someone else's established site, you'll be able to get the word out about your website.
>
> **Search Engine Optimization (SEO).** SEO will also be important in directing people to your website. If you're not very familiar with SEO, I suggest that you take some time to read a few articles on SEO and what you can do to optimize your website in internet

searches. If you don't have the time to do this, you might consider hiring an SEO marketing expert to do this for you.

Paid advertising. Another option you can use to drive people to your website is paid advertising. Social media sites generally offer affordable ads. Or you can buy banner ads on small niche sites that are related to your niche. GoogleAdWords might also be a good option for you, depending on your niche.

Make Money Dropshipping

Dropshipping is yet another way for you to make passive income. For those of you who are not exactly sure what dropshipping is, let me provide a description that may help. Dropshipping is a retail fulfillment method in which you will be able to sell the retail products of your choice on an online store which you create. The benefit of dropshipping for you is that you will not need to open a brick-and-mortar store with its large overhead and monthly lease and insurance costs. You won't have to hire and pay employees or do payroll taxes. You won't have to carry or stock any merchandise. All of that will be handled by a third party, a supplier who will store and warehouse the items you're selling and who will ship the items you sell directly to the consumer.

You'll be responsible for securing sales for the items you are selling. You will also be able to set prices on these items, but those prices will have to be comparable to what the market dictates or offered by competitors or companies selling the same merchandise. It should be pointed out that with dropshipping programs, the products you are selling are likely to be sold by other companies as well, so your pricing will probably need to remain competitive and you might find that your profit margins will be slim, depending on the item.

Let me take you through how this process works behind the scenes. Let's say that I have an online store that sells custom minor league baseball jerseys. All of these jerseys contain the logos and designs of different minor league baseball teams. A customer purchases a jersey from my website for $40 and pays me online for that jersey. I then forward the order to my supplier or wholesaler, who is selling the jersey to me for $28. The supplier then sends the order to the customer using a shipping label with my name on it. This "blind label" is used so the customer will recognize the shipper of the item. It is also used so the customer will not be able to bypass me and go directly to the supplier or wholesaler. When the supplier or wholesaler ships the jersey to the customer, they will charge me for the $32 cost of the jersey plus shipping. So, my role in the entire sale is simple: I secured the sale and sent it to the supplier, and I sent an acknowledgment to the customer. The supplier made, stored, and shipped the jersey. I also collected a cool $8 for the sale. All in all, as an affiliate marketer, I am a middleman. As you can see, dropshipping is a simple business model that requires a minimal investment in time and money on your part. If you find the right niche and the right supplier, dropshipping can be a profitable venture.

Five Essential Steps in Creating Dropshipping Business

Here are five essential steps for achieving dropshipping success.

1) **Find a niche.** We've discussed how important it is to find a niche in the previous sections on blogging and affiliate marketing. The same principles apply here. If you're going to get involved in dropshipping, you'll be involved in a venue in which you're likely to have many competitors. With this in

mind, the more you are able to refine your niche, the more successful you'll be. For example, if you want to fine-tune your niche, you can go from pet products down to dog products down to puppy products or dog training products, etc. You get the picture. The more you fine-tune your niche, the fewer your competitors and the higher your profit margins will be.

2) **Research your competition.** Speaking of competition, it will be important for you to research your competition to find out how much they are charging for the same or similar items you intend to sell on your site. This should give you an idea of the profit margins that will be involved with the items you're intending to sell. If you discover that you'll have to sell for low margins on most of the items you intend to sell, you might want to rethink the niche you have chosen.

3) **Select a platform.** With your dropshipping business, you'll have plenty of platforms to choose from. I'll outline three of the most popular platforms here to give you a good idea of what is available to you.

>**Doba** has a huge selection of products and suppliers for you to use in your dropshipping activities. They have over 2 million products to choose from. These products come from nearly 200 suppliers. In working with Doba, you will not have to partner with multiple dropshippers. Doba charges $29 a month for its basic program and a 99 cents per order fee. They have live training webinars for newbies and they'll send you email updates regarding supplier discounts, new

products and seasonal products, and new suppliers as they become available to you.

Oberlo is a platform which is tightly integrated with Shopify. It allows for easy one-click import of AliExpress products. Please know that Oberlo works only with Shopify stores and it only supports AliExpress for now. They offer a free account, but with the free account, you will be limited to 500 products and 50 orders per month. When your orders exceed 50 orders a month, your monthly fee will go to $29.90.

Dropship Direct has over 100,000 items from more than 900 brands for you to choose from. It's free to use, but as you grow your business, you'll note that they have a back-end management system that is available for $37/month or free to those who are doing over $1000 a month in sales.

Other dropship platforms that might merit a look include **Wholesale2B, Megagoods, SaleHoo, Sunrise Wholesale, Wholesale Central, and National Dropshipper.**

4) **Build your ecommerce site.** After you've determined which platform you're going to use for your dropshipping activities, you'll need to develop a website or a store on which to sell the products you've chosen. Most dropshipping newbies use Shopify for their ecommerce store. Shopify has a web-based site builder that will allow you to get your dropshipping business up and running quickly. You won't need a tech background to launch a website on Shopify. And with a Shopify site, you'll have complete control over your site's

navigation, content pages, and design. Also, Shopify has a built-in payment processing system that will allow you to accept payments from customers who are purchasing items on your site. And Shopify has multiple apps which will help you in developing a successful dropshipping business. Additionally, Shopify has a number of pricing plans for you to choose from. Those plans start at $29/month and Shopify will take 2.9% of sales and 30 cents per transaction on top of the monthly fee.

5) **Drive people to your site.** Once you have your ecommerce site up and running, your work isn't finished. You're going to have to continue to work to get people to visit your site. You'll do this on social media, in your blogs and vlogs, and with emails. I have outlined most of these marketing activities in the chapter on affiliate marketing, so I won't repeat them here. But I do emphasize the importance of making people aware of your site, not just once, but on a continual basis. If you have good products to sell at reasonable prices, the key to growing your business will revolve around your ability to get people to visit that site.

Chapter 5—Get Richer While You Sleep

In this chapter, I'm going to show you some additional passive income streams to help you earn even more money while you sleep. Maybe you can even get to a point where you'll be making so much money while you sleep that you'll want to sleep all the time. Just kidding. (joke)

Amazon FBA

Amazon FBA stands for Fulfillment By Amazon. Amazon FBA has become one of the most popular ways to earn income online. There are almost 2 million people selling on Amazon worldwide. About half of the sales on Amazon come from third-party selling; of the top 10,000 Amazon sellers, about two-thirds of those sellers use FBA.

Here's how it works. You send your products to Amazon. They stock them and store them for you. When a customer orders one of your products, Amazon then picks, packs, ships, and tracks that product for you. They also handle all returns and refunds. Amazon then pays you every two weeks for any of the merchandise you have sold. In return for their efforts, Amazon charges storage fees and fulfillment fees.

There are a number of major advantages to using Amazon FBA to sell your items. Most importantly, they offer you immediate access to millions of potential customers. Over 300 million people have purchased from Amazon; they have over 90 million Amazon Prime members. Bottom line, no other company can even come close to offering you access to this many customers. And because of all the packages it ships and all the warehouses it has in different parts of the country, Amazon is able to ship and deliver items less expensively than anyone else. One of the biggest reasons people use Amazon is because of the free shipping they offer to their Prime customers and also to their non-Prime customers who place orders that achieve a minimum dollar amount. Also, Amazon is well-known for its prompt shipping, its great customer service, and its generous return policy. All of these things have allowed Amazon to build its reputation as a retailer, and the volume that Amazon generates shows the confidence that consumers have in the company.

If you're going to use Amazon FBA, you should be aware of the various fees associated with it. If you're just getting started, Amazon has an individual plan for those people who sell less than 40 items per month. There is no subscription fee for this plan. (Item-selling fees obviously still apply.) If you're selling more than 40 items a month on Amazon, the next step up is their professional selling plan, which has a monthly subscription charge of $39.99. (Again, item selling fees apply.) Individual plan sellers on Amazon pay a fee of .99 per item sold and variable closing fees of .45 to $1.35 per item. Professional sellers pay variable closing fees and referral fees ranging from 6% to 25%, averaging 13%.

If you're going to participate in Amazon's FBA program, you'll pay storage fees for Amazon to store your items in its warehouse. There are short-term and long-term storage fees. Short-term fees are monthly fees that vary depending on the time of the year the items are stored. From January through September, you have to pay about .65 per cubic foot; during the holiday season, October through December, you have to pay $2.40 per cubic foot. In addition to that, you'll need to pay long-term storage fees for any of your items which Amazon stores for over a year. Amazon takes what they call an inventory cleanup every February 15 and August 15 and they'll then notify you of any items you've had in their inventory for over a year. But you can avoid long-term storage fees if you submit a removal order and get those items out of the Amazon warehouse. Thus long-term storage fees should not be a major concern. Either way, it will also behoove you to stay on top of your inventory so you can minimize monthly storage fees and eliminate the possibility of any long-term fees.

In reviewing Amazon FBA success stories, I've noted that the biggest success stories involve sellers who are selling unique products or product niches. If you want to get rich selling through Amazon FBA, you'll want to have an extremely unique product, possibly even an item or concept that you have created. For example, Amazon FBA success stories include a man who created a toy card game and another man who created a concept on flipping used books for a profit. Still another man took an old concept that had lost steam and marketed it to a new audience. He took a pop-up basketball hoop and net that had previously sold in arcades, fairs, and bars, and remarketed it so it was targeted for home use. Someone else worked with a Chinese manufacturer to develop a line of ultra-comfortable shoes, while another scouted and made available a line of health products for pet lovers. And yet another selected trendy items that he could privately label and made them available. As you can see, most of these success stories involve unique products or concepts. If you have an item like this or if you can find one, you could have tremendous success on Amazon FBA.

All You Need to Know About Peer-to-Peer Lending Opportunities

Peer-to-peer (P2P) lending is another way you can make passive income, by using your money to make more money. For those of you unfamiliar with peer-to-peer lending, let me describe it to you.

With P2P lending, individuals loan their money to individuals or small businesses that are looking to borrow money. In essence, P2P is non-bank lending which cuts out the middleman—the banks. P2P lending has become attractive to yield-seeking investors who are looking for alternatives to replace lower yield traditional investments such as savings, bonds, money market funds, and certificates of deposit.

If you're saying that you don't have money to invest, I should point out quickly that you won't have to invest large amounts. Many popular P2P lending companies, including Prosper and Lending Club, require a minimum investment of only $25 in each loan. Peer-to-peer lending generally offers a rate of return that ranges from 5 to 11%. P2P lending is generally considered safe, but, as with any lending, there is some risk involved, as the loans offered are unsecured loans.

Here's how P2P lending works. A person (or business) looking to borrow money goes to a P2P lending site and fills out an application that includes the reason they want to borrow money and the amount they are looking for. P2P loans range from $1000 to $35,000. That information is then made available to prospective investors who can choose what loans they invest in. Loans are priced and categorized based on numerous factors, including the prospective borrower's credit score, current income level, the requested loan amount, and the desired term of the loan. It's important to note that almost all lending platforms do not entertain sub-prime borrowers. In fact, most of the lending platforms require a minimum credit score of 600 to 650 and they typically don't make loans to people or businesses that have had recent bankruptcies, judgments, or tax liens.

With P2P lending, the platform handles all of the administrative tasks involved in the loans, including underwriting, closing, distribution of the loan, and collection of the monthly payments. In return for that, the lending platforms take a management fee (usually 1%) for their role in administrating the loan. This management fee is subtracted from each monthly payment. With P2P lending, all the investor has to do is to select the loans they want to invest in.

As mentioned above, there is some risk in investing in P2P loans. The main risk is the possibility of default. As these are unsecured loans, you could stand to lose the money you've invested if the borrower defaults on the loan. And there is no FDIC insurance on these loans. So, worst-case scenario, the money you invest in P2P lending could decrease instead of increase. Another thing to remember is that these investments have limited liquidity. So, once you've invested, you probably won't be able to get your money out until the term of the loan has expired.

In going into the details of the possible risks of P2P lending investment, I don't do so to discourage you from participating in this form of investment. I just want you to beware of the possible pitfalls which are associated with P2P lending. Most lending platforms will rank the risk involved with each loan and some of the platforms allow you to invest in all of their different risk categories. This allows the investor to diversify his portfolio and the offset higher risks with lower risks.

I've listed some of the most popular lending platforms for investors with a brief description for each:

 Prosper is one of the most popular P2P lending platforms. It allows investors to invest a minimum of $25 in a loan. Prosper has seven different risk categories that have estimated returns ranging from about 5% to 13-1/2%. It allows investors to spread their risks out over all categories so they can diversify their portfolios and balance their overall risks.

Lending Tree is another popular site. With Lending Tree, you can invest as little as $25 in any loan, but you'll still need to transfer a minimum of $1000 into your account. With this platform, if you don't want to select loans manually, they'll let you choose a platform mix or a custom mix.

Peerform has 16 different risk categories. They allow investors to invest in whole loans or fractional loans. Also, they'll allow you to spread your loans over the different risk categories, so you can diversify your portfolio and average out your risks at a level you're comfortable with.

Here are some other popular platforms you might be interested in: Upstart, StreetShares, FoundingCircle, and Kiva. StreetShares and FundingCircle target small business loans. Kiva targets loans for non-profit organizations.

40 Ways You Can Use Your Skills or Interests to Earn Passive Income

This will be fun. In rapid-fire fashion, I'm going to throw out some quick ideas on how you might use your skills or interests to earn passive income. I won't spend a lot of time or space on these ideas, as that would take an entire book itself. However, I'm hoping that at least some of these ideas will be helpful to you. I offer a wide range of ideas and I'm offering them randomly. You'll realize immediately that some of the ideas are not for you, but hopefully some of them will spark some interest for you.

1) **Take Online Surveys.** You can make money in your spare time by completing surveys online. There are lots of online

research firms that will pay you to complete surveys. Start with **Survey Junkie** and then if you still have extra time, register with other companies.
2) **Freelance Writer.** Are you a writer? If so, you can make extra cash by writing articles, blogs, books, web copy, etc. Start with **Upwork** and **Contently.**
3) **Freelance Editor.** Are you good at editing? If so, you can make money editing blogs, thesis papers, articles, web copy, books, etc. Again, start with **Upwork** and **Contently.**
4) **Paint Houses.** Do you like painting? Are you good at it? If so, you should be able to make some extra cash painting houses, inside or out. Your client buys the paint, but you'll have to supply the other necessary materials.
5) **Sell Your College Class Notes.** If you take good notes, you can probably make some extra money by selling notes to students who are taking the same classes the following semester.
6) **Sell Your Plasma.** I did this when I was in college. Unlike blood, which can be donated only every eight weeks, you can sell your plasma up to twice a week, at $25 to $50 per session. If you have a plasma center near you, this is a great way to earn extra cash. Most cities now have plasma centers. If you are attending a large university, there is almost certainly a plasma center nearby.
7) **Sell Your Photographs.** Are you a good photographer? Do you like to take photos? Well, you can sell those photos to stock photo sites and you can sell the same photo again and again. Who buys these stock photos? People buy them to use on websites, in blogs and newsletters, on book covers, etc. It's expensive to hire a photographer, and many people prefer to instead purchase photos from a stock photo site. Start with **istockphoto, SmugMug Pro,** and **Shutterstock.**

8) **Make, Grow, Sell Things at Farmer's Markets.** Do you have a farmer's market in your community or a surrounding community? If so, these are great places to sell lots of homegrown or homemade items, including fruits and veggies, baked goods, crafts, quilts, and homemade honey, syrup, or salsa. Check out the nearby farmer's market and see if it offers you the possibility of selling any of your homegrown or homemade items.

9) **Sports Tutor.** Are you knowledgeable about sports? If so, you might consider being a sports tutor. If you are a good baseball player, you might consider offering your services to teach kids how to improve their hitting skills. Were you a quarterback in high school or college? Teach aspiring quarterbacks how to improve their throwing skills. Tennis? Soccer? Gymnastics? Many parents are willing to spend money to have their kids improve their sports skills.

10) **Math Tutor.** Along the same lines, if you're good at mathematics you can sell your services as a math tutor. I have a daughter that did that for middle school kids and she earned some nice part-time income tutoring kids in math.

11) **Second Language Tutor.** Again, along the same lines, if you are proficient at a second language, you can teach/tutor students to learn another language. And with all these tutoring ideas, you should note that you can do that tutoring in person or online, individually or in group sessions. A friend of mine has a son who is paying for his post-college trip across Europe by teaching English to Chinese students online.

12) **Voice-Over Work.** Do you have a good voice? If so, you can earn extra money doing freelance voice-over work. Start with **Upwork** or **Fiverr** to find your gigs.

13) **Get Paid to Shop.** Many people now use personal shoppers for a variety of reasons. Some people use personal shoppers to do their holiday gift shopping (I saw that in a Hallmark movie). My neighbor lady is 92 years old and she pays a woman to do her weekly grocery shopping. Some corporate executives who don't have much time to spare will hire someone to run errands, such as picking up dry cleaning.
14) **Handyman Gigs.** Good handymen are hard to find. If you're good at fixing things around the house, you should consider hiring yourself out as a handyman. Start with **Angie's List, Takl,** or a classified ad in your local newspaper.
15) **Housecleaning.** You can earn extra cash by hiring yourself out as a housecleaner, either on a continual basis, such as once a week, or you can sell your services to people who are moving and may not have time to clean their places properly before leaving. Again, start with **Angie's List and Takl.**
16) **Housesitting.** Yes, some people will let you live in their homes for free if they are going to be gone for extended periods of time. No parties, please.
17) **Yard Work Services.** Some people are not interested, not able, or don't have the time to do their own yard work. You can fill the void by mowing the lawn, shoveling snow, cleaning gutters, raking leaves, trimming bushes, etc.
18) **Sewing Services.** Are you good with a sewing machine? Can you mend clothes or shorten a pair of trousers? If so, you can make extra money at home sewing. Also, please note that some people make extra cash ironing or pressing clothes from their homes.
19) **Babysitting.** A great way for a responsible high schooler or college student to earn some extra cash.
20) **Pet Sitting.** Along the same lines, many pet owners don't know what to do with their pets when they are going away

and can't take their pets with them, as the rising popularity of pet hotels shows. If you're a pet lover, this is a good way to earn some extra income. Put the word out.

21) **Dog Walking.** Yes, some people don't have the time to walk their dogs. This offers you an opportunity to make some money and get some exercise at the same time.

22) **Teach Exercise Classes.** If you're an exercise buff, you can earn extra income teaching exercise classes such as spinning, yoga, Zumba, CrossFit, etc. Make money while staying in great shape.

23) **Phone-A-Friend/Welfare Check.** One of my neighbors started a company in which she does a daily welfare check on elderly persons. She has assembled a nice roster of clients and calls each person at the same time every day. Her services are mostly paid for by the daughters or sons of the elderly person who are concerned about the welfare of the elderly parent.

24) **Crafts.** Are you good or could you be good at a particular craft? If you handmake jewelry, leather goods, clothing, etc., you can sell your items on various crafts platforms. Start with **Etsy** as the place to sell your items.

25) **Small Engine and Motor Repair.** Are you good at fixing small engines? Lawnmowers, snowblowers, boat motors? If so, there's money to be made in doing so. Same goes for simple appliances such as washers, dryers, refrigerators, etc.

26) **Photography.** Are you good with a camera? If so, you might hire yourself out for special events such as weddings, anniversary celebrations, proms, family holiday card photos, family pet photos, etc.

27) **Music Lessons, Musical Instrument Lessons.** Are you a good vocalist? Good at the piano, the drums, the guitar? Earn

extra cash by giving lessons to people trying to become better singers or musicians.

28) **Dance Instructor.** Are you a good enough dancer to be able to teach it? Are you good enough to offer lessons to a couple who wants to learn or refine their dancing before their wedding day?

29) **Mystery Shopping.** Many national retail companies have mystery shopping programs in which they will send an anonymous mystery shopper to see how their customers are being treated. You can get paid to visit restaurants and retail locations. Start with **Best Mark** or **Market Force** to see what mystery shopping opportunities are available in your area.

30) **Window Cleaning.** This is another job that people will pay other people to do. Window cleaning requires a minimal amount of tools.

31) **Computer, Electronic Device Repair.** Are you good at this? Many people are willing to pay a nice fee for someone to repair their computer or other electronic devices. A lot of times, these are very simple problems and the customer simply isn't tech-savvy.

32) **Caricature Artist, Face Painter.** My niece is very talented at drawing caricatures. She can sketch a caricature in about 10 minutes and would often take her easel and pencil to various major events around town and offer to do sketches, for a fee of course. She did that at major concerts and sporting events. Also, she went to the beach on days when a lot of people were there and offered to do caricature sketches. Along the same lines, she learned how to face paint and then used that skill to make extra money at college football games.

33) **Design T-Shirts.** Do you have a knack for coming up with designs for things like t-shirts, bumper stickers, coffee mugs,

etc.? If so, check out CafePress. You can place your designs for sale on that site; and then, when customers order a t-shirt with one of your designs, you'll earn a portion of the profits. CafePress will ship the item to the customer and collect the money. You won't have to do a thing other than to load the design.

34) **Private Cooking Lessons.** Are you a great cook? If so, you can earn some extra cash by teaching other people how to cook. Maybe some people will just want to learn the basics of cooking. Others might want to learn how to make desserts or bake pies. Others might want a crash course in Italian cooking or French cooking. You get the picture. You can make extra money teaching others what you're already good at.

35) **Organize Homes or Offices.** Are you good at organizing things? You can help people get rid of the clutter in their homes and offices.

36) **Website Design.** Are you an expert at web design? If so, your skillset offers you a great opportunity to earn extra cash. And you can do it all on the internet. Looking to get some web design gigs? Start with **Upwork** and **Fiverr.**

37) **Drive for Cash.** Do you have a reliable car? Know how to get around in the city you live in? You can make money by driving people to their destination. Many of you have heard of **Uber** or **Lyft.** If you'd rather not drive people around, there is an on-demand delivery service called **Postmate** in which you will be paid to deliver groceries, restaurant meals, liquor store orders, etc.

38) **Videographer.** Have a video cam? Good at turning pictures into videos? Then you should be able to make cash as a videographer. Start with special events like wedding

receptions, birthday parties, anniversaries, family and class reunions, etc.

39) **Graphic Design Services.** Most small businesses can't afford expensive ad agencies to design their various marketing materials. But if you are proficient at graphic design, you have the opportunity to earn extra cash as a designer. You should be able to find some design gigs on **99 Designs.**

40) **Home Staging.** Can you make a home look attractive, inviting, and welcoming? It's common knowledge that staged or decorated homes sell much faster and for more money than empty homes. If you enjoy doing this, contact your local real estate agencies to see if they would be interested in this service. You'll also have no problem in working for multiple agencies, as the homes will already be listed by a specific real estate agency by the time the house is staged.

Chapter 6--Make Killer Investments

In this chapter, I'll provide you with beginner's information on three other passive income revenue streams: stocks, CDs (certificates of deposit), and real estate. I'm detailing these passive income opportunities in the final chapter of the book, as, in most instances, these are "use money to make more money" opportunities. Although large amounts of money are not required for any of these activities, you'll need to at least have some money to start with to participate in these investment opportunities.

How to Start Investing in Stocks

If you've never invested in stocks, it's important for you to know that investing in stocks isn't as complicated as it might seem. There are now many easy to use tools available to help you invest in stocks, whether you want to take a hands-on or hands-off approach. If you're considering investing in stocks, one of the most important things to remember is that investing in stocks is a long-term game. It's not meant to be a get-rich-quick scheme. In other words, you shouldn't invest money in stocks that you might need in the short term. This includes any emergency funds you might have tucked away. The reason for this is that many stock investments will fluctuate and, if you need to get out of these investments because you need cash for other things, you'll be subject to wherever the market is at that time. And, if the market or your stocks are down, you may even lose money on your original investment. It's been proven that most stock investments will continue to increase in value over time, but the market will fluctuate and you'll want to make sure you're not in a position where you have to withdraw your funds when the market and your investments are tracking down. As a rule of thumb, you should be comfortable parting with your money for at least five years. Why five years? That's because history shows that even if the market takes a downturn, it's very unlikely that a downturn would last longer than five years.

If you've yet to invest in the stock market and you're wondering if you can invest even if you don't have much money, the answer is yes, although there are some challenges. These challenges can be overcome, but you need to be aware of them before you begin investing. The first challenge to overcome is that many stock investments require a minimum. The second challenge involves diversification. With stock investing strategies, it's common practice to diversify your investments so you will not have "all your eggs in one basket". If you have limited funds, it's going to be difficult to spread your limited funds around.

The solution to both of these challenges is to invest in stock index funds and ETFs (exchange-traded funds). For those of you not familiar with exchange-traded funds, you should know that ETFs are investment funds traded on the stock exchange, much like stocks. ETFs hold assets such as stocks, commodities, or bonds. While mutual funds might require a minimum investment of $1000 or more, stock index fund minimums tend to be lower and ETFs tend to be even lower than index funds. As a matter of fact, some brokers offer index funds with no minimum at all. (Fidelity and Charles Schwab are two of the brokers that offer index funds without minimums.) So, not only are index funds available without minimums, they also have a built-in solution to the diversification problem, as index funds consist of many different stocks within a single fund.

If you're interested in receiving a passive income stream for your stock investments without having to sell the stocks you've invested in, you might consider dividend stocks, stocks that pay dividends. Well-established companies such as Target, Pepsico, Exxon, or Disney are more likely to pay dividends than some of the newer and less-established companies. The more established companies no longer need to invest all of their profits into growing the company and they can afford to pay out profits to their investors. On the other hand, newer companies, especially tech or biotech companies, are a lot less likely to pay out dividends, as they want to use as much of their profit as possible to expand the company.

There are two main types of dividends—cash dividends and stock dividends. These dividends are often paid quarterly, although some are paid monthly or semi-annually. Dividends offer a way for companies to distribute revenue back to investors and one of the ways investors earn a return from investing in the stock. Cash dividends are paid per each share of stock that you own. For example, if you own 20 shares in a company's stock and that company pays $2 in annual dividends, you will receive $40 per year for your stock shares. Some companies pay stock dividends instead of cash dividends, so instead of getting cash from your investment, you'll receive additional company stock. You'll then be able to sell that stock if you wish to get cash or you'll be able to keep it invested in the company. Some companies offer dividend reinvestments programs, called DRIPs, in which investors are allowed to reinvest their dividends back into the company's stock, often at a discounted rate. So, if you are interested in receiving a passive income stream from your stock investments, you'll want to specifically choose dividend stocks for your portfolio.

Now that I've given you some basic information on stocks, you should be ready to start investing. Here are some simple steps to get you started:

Determine if you're going to be a hands-on or hands-off investor. If you want to be heavily involved in choosing the stocks you invest in, you're going to need a stockbroker. I'm going to recommend three different brokers that are well-suited for beginning investors:

1) **Merrill Edge.** A good choice for beginning stock investors, as no minimum deposit is required. Charges $6.95 per trade.
2) **TD Ameritrade.** Another good choice for beginners. Like Merrill Edge, no minimum deposit required and a $6.95 charge per trade. Currently running a promotion in which trade charges are waived for 60 days, but with a qualifying deposit. With any broker you're considering, please check their sites to see what promotions they are offering. These promotional offers are always subject to change, so what's offered one month might next be available the next month.
3) **E-Trade** requires a minimum account balance of $500, but they also have a promotion offering a cash credit, up to $600, for a qualifying account deposit. $6.95 charge per trade.

If you don't want to be heavily involved in selecting the stocks you invest in, you should consider using a robo-advisor account instead of a stockbroker. Most major brokerages offer robo-advisors, as they are extremely cost-efficient for the casual investor. In using a robo-advisor, you can get all the benefits of stock investing without having to do all the research you would have to do if you selected the stocks that you wanted to invest in. Robo-advisor services cover complete investment management. When you go to register for a robo-advisor, you'll be asked a series of questions regarding your investment goals. From that information, the robo-advisor will build a portfolio that fits with your goals and objectives. Here are three different robo-advisors which are well-suited for beginning investors:

1) **Wealthfront.** $500 account minimum with a 0.25% management fee. Please note that the 0.25% management fee is substantially less than you would pay a human investment manager.
2) **Betterment.** No account minimum with a 0.25% management fee that can be free for up to a year with a qualifying deposit.
3) **SoFi.** $100 account minimum with 0% management fees.

One other note before we move on from stocks to CDs: One of the best stock investment options for beginners is mutual funds. Mutual funds offer an easy and low-cost way for you to get your feet wet in the stock market. An S & P 500 fund is a great place to start. For those of you that have heard the term S & P fund, but don't know what it means, an S & P fund is a fund consisting of stocks from the 500 largest US companies. If you invest in an S & P fund, you'll be purchasing a small slice of 500 of the country's most successful companies. As these companies are already proven entities, you'll be investing in a group of companies that is likely to continue to thrive.

In a similar vein, if you are using a robo-advisor, the advisor will be able to create a portfolio of stocks from successful companies with which you'll be able to own a sliver of each of these customers and diversify your portfolio. These are low-risk stock investments, as the companies you'll be invested in will be proven entities.

All About CD Laddering

Before we get into CD laddering, I'll define what a CD is. A CD is a certificate of deposit. It is a time deposit that is commonly sold by banks, credit unions, or thrift institutions. CDs offer a very low-risk alternative to people who are looking to get higher interest rates than the meager interest rates they get on their savings accounts. The trade-off is that with a savings account you can generally take out your money at any time without a withdrawal penalty. With a CD, you will not be able to access your money for the length of the deposit, whether it is a one-year deposit or a five-year deposit.

CD laddering is a very simple process. CD laddering involves purchasing multiple CDs at the same time, with each CD maturing at different times. e.g., 1-year, 3-year, 5-year. Instead of placing all of your CD money in the same time interval, you will choose different intervals. CD laddering offers total flexibility. You can purchase different amounts for different intervals; you can even choose different banks for your different CDs, depending on the interest rates offered by those different banks. For example, if you have $10,000 to invest in CDs, you could invest $3000 in a 1-year CD, $3000 in a 2-year CD, $2000 in a 3-year CD, and $2000 in a 5-year CD. Maybe you use one bank for the l- and 2-year CDs and another bank for the 3- and 5-year CDs because they are offering a higher interest rate than the first bank is offering on those intervals.

CDs already guarantee a rate of return. By laddering, you can get even higher interest rates and you'll always be close to having money that is available for any unexpected emergencies.

Let me give you another example to show how you can earn additional interest by laddering your CDS. Again, let's say you have $10,000 to invest in CDs. If you invest all $10,000 in 1-year CDs and continue to roll those CDs over as they mature, on an annual percentage yield of 2.8%, you will have increased your $10,000 to $11,502.68 in a 10-year period. On the other hand, if you take that same $10,000, and invest $2000 each in 1-,2-,3-,4-, and 5-year CDs, you'll get the higher interest rates as the length of the term increases. If you are getting the 2.8% interest on a 1-year, 2.95% on a 2-year, 3% on a 3-year, 3.05% on a 4-year, and 3.15% on a 5-year, you original $10,000 will have increased to $11,668.36 after 10 years.

Four Simple Ways to Make Real Estate Investment Income

Investing in real estate offers lucrative opportunities for you to earn additional passive income. One of the exciting things about investing in real estate properties is that, unlike stocks and bonds, you can pay for just a portion of your real estate investment before you can begin making money from it. Normally, you'll pay 20 to 25% as a down payment for the real estate you purchase. In some instances, you might even pay as low as 5%. Regardless of what your percentage is, from the time you sign your mortgage papers, you'll be able to start earning money from that investment.

Let's look at four simple ways you can make money from your real estate investments:

1) **Become a landlord.** If you buy a house or a small commercial property, you'll be able to make money by renting out that property. The upside of this is obvious. You'll be able to use your renter's payments to pay your mortgage. In many instances, you will be charging your renters a monthly rent that is more than your monthly mortgage payments. So, not

only can you make money on your monthly payments from a renter, you can also use them to make your mortgage payments and increase your equity in the property as the property is probably appreciating.

In all fairness, there are some possible negatives involved in being a landlord. Unless you pay a company to manage your property, you'll be stuck with handling any problems at that property. If the hot water heater goes out, you'll be responsible for replacing it as soon as possible. If the washing machine, stops working, you have to either get it fixed or replace it...in most instances, at your expense. If you rent to bad tenants, it's possible that they can damage or destroy your property. If they don't pay their monthly rent, you're still going to have to make your mortgage payment and you might even have to pay to evict those tenants. If you can't rent your property and it's vacant, you're still going to have to make the mortgage payment.

That said, if you ever get to a point where your mortgage is paid off, the rent you collect will become almost all profit. At the same time, as you own the property for a period of time, that property is probably going to appreciate and you'll have a much more valuable asset than you started with.

2) **Real estate investment groups** are a great option for people who want to own real estate but don't want the hassles of being a landlord or managing a property. In a typical real estate group, a company buys or builds a set of apartment buildings or a condominium complex. They then allow people to purchase the units within those building or complexes. A person who buys a unit then becomes part of the real estate investment group. A single investor can own

one or multiple units in the buildings or complexes, but the company operating the investment group will continue to manage all units, handle all maintenance, advertise vacancies, and secure tenants, in return for a certain percentage of the monthly rent. If you are in a real estate group and your particular unit has a vacancy, you'll still receive a monthly payment, as any vacancies will be covered by the entire investment group. As long as there are not a lot of vacancies in the building or complex, you should still be able to derive monthly income from the unit(s) you own.

3) **Real estate trading (flipping).** This is the wild side of real estate investing. Real estate trading is very risky, but it can also be extremely lucrative. Flipping is not for the "weak of heart". If you're going to be successful at flipping, you are most likely going to have to be good at evaluating real estate and then marketing that real estate. There are two types of flippers. The pure flipper is interested in buying properties that require very little or no alteration. They will simply want to resell the property for more than they paid for it. The other type of flipper buys reasonably priced properties with the idea of renovating them or improving them to a point where they can then be resold at a profit. This is often a longer process than pure flipping, but profits can be substantial. If you're going to do this type of flipping, you're going to have to be willing to secure contractors who can renovate the property and you're going to have to be willing to oversee this work. Some people get into flipping without an idea of who to hire or what it is going to cost to make the improvements they want to make to give the property more value. If you've been hooked on the TV shows that revolve around house flipping or if you've been reading some of the

tremendous success stories regarding flipping, you should know there are also many stories out there concerning newbies who expected to make their fortunes by flipping homes, but got in over their heads and had a disastrous flipping experience

4) **Real estate investment trusts (REITs)** are basically a more formalized version of real estate investment groups. A REIT is created when a corporation (or trust) uses investor money to buy and operate income properties. Unlike the aforementioned real estate investment groups, REITS include non-residential properties or real estate ventures, such as shopping centers, malls, and office complexes. REITs are bought and sold on the major exchanges, just like stock. With REITs, a corporation must pay out 90% of its excess profits to investors as dividends in order to maintain its REIT status. In doing this, REITs do not have to pay corporate income taxes, whereas a regular company would be taxed on its profits and then have to decide whether or not to issue dividends to investors from its after-tax profits. REITs are considered to be a solid investment for investors who want regular income.

Conclusion

Is there a better time than now to start earning more money? With all the passive income streams I've provided you in this book, you can no longer say that you don't have any ideas as to how you can earn some extra money. No one would ever pretend that all of these ideas will suit you, however there are definitely some ideas that you can pursue. Now the question is, are you going to spend your time complaining that you don't have any extra income streams or are you going to do something about it? I've given you the tools to be successful. What you do with those tools is up to you. When you were a kid and got a brand-new toy for your birthday, did you wait to use that new toy? I'll guess that you started playing with that new toy immediately. The same goes for the ideas in this book. Surely, you found at least a few good ideas among all the options I presented. Excuse the analogy, but now that you've read this book, the bus has just dropped you off at the road to success. Are you going to get on that road or are you going to get back on the bus?

Whether you use your money to make more money or whether you simply use your skills to make money, it's time to start now. I doubt that you would have read this book if you were not interested in making more money. Yes, most of the ideas presented will require some time or effort on your part. However, if you are willing to put in the initial effort, many of the ideas presented will allow you to earn extra money, some of it while you sleep. Checking your bank account balance can become something you look forward to instead of something you'd rather not do at all.

Whether you embark on micro-investing, blogging, peer-to-peer lending, or just walking dogs, there's no better time than now for you to start earning more money.

Resources

Chapter 1.

Brassfield, Mike. (Updated August 1, 2019). "A Beginner's Guide to Micro-Investing".
https://www.thepennyhoarder.com/investing/how-to-start-micro-investing/

Chapter 2.

Hussain, Anum. (November 28, 2018). "How to Create an Ebook from Start to Finish". https:/blog.hubspot.com/marketing/how-to-create-an-ebook-free-templates/

Bolt, Chandler. (August 2, 2019). "Your Guide on How to Make Money with Ebooks". https://www.nichepursuits.com/guide-to-make-money-ebooks/

Bolt, Chandler. (July 30, 2019). "How to Make an Audio Book Step-by-Step". https://self-publishingschool.com/creating-audio-book-every-author-know/

(Author name, date not available) https://socialtriggers.com/online-courses-create-and-sell/

Chapter 3.

Knapp, Jessica. (December 26, 2017). "How to Make Money with Your Blog in 2019". https://www.bloggingbasics101.com/how-can-i-make-money-from-my-blog/

Peterson, Sarah. (Updated May 31, 2019). "7 Totally Legitimate Ways to Make Passive Income from Your Blog".
https://smartblogger.com/ways -to-make-passive-income/

Morrow, Jon. (Updated August 15, 2019). "How to Make Money Blogging. (Free Guide for 2019)". https://smartblogger.com/make-money-blogging/

Lohana, Pooja. (Date not available.) "6 Ways to Make Money with Advertising on Your Blog and the Websites to Help You". https://www.jeffbullas.com/blog/-advertising/

Chapter 4.

Enfroy, Adam. (Date not available) "Affiliate Marketing in 2019. What It Is and How You Can Get Started". https://www.bigcommerce.com/blog/affiliate-marketing/

(Author name not available) (February 21, 2019). "Affiliate Marketing: 5 Successful Strategies for Beginners". https://www.renderforest.com/blog/affiliate-marketing-trends-2019/

Long, Jonathon. (May 16, 2019). "6 Steps to Building a Successful Online Dropshipping Business". https://www.entrepreneur.com/article/297744

(Author name, date not available). "Dropshipping 101: Ecommerce without Inventory". https://www.my.oberlo.com/blog/dropshipping-niches/

Basuthakur, Radhika. (October 17, 2018). "Affiliate Marketing for Beginners: How to Make Your First Affiliate Marketing Sale in 7 Steps". https://affilorama.com/blog/first-affiliate-marketing-sale/

Chapter 5.

Spencer, Jamie. (Updated July 15, 2019). "How to Make a Website". https://makeawebsitehub.com/start-amazon-fba-business/

Ravia. (November 28, 2018). "8 Best Dropshipping Companies for Your Ecommerce Business". https://emergeapp.net/drop-shipping/8-best-drop-shipping-companies/

Carragher, Gennifer. (Date not available.) "How to Leverage the Power of Amazon FBA". https://bigcommerce.com/blog/amazon-fba/#how-amazon-fba-works/

Hufford, Jillian. (August 19, 2019). "Are Fulfillment by Amazon's (FBA) Fees Worth the Cost". https://nchannel.com/blog/is-fulfillment-by-amazon-fba-worth-the-cost/

Mercadante, Kevin. (Updated April 7, 2019). "Should You Invest in Peer-to-Peer Loans". https://moneyunder30.com/invest-in-peer-to-peer-loans/

Muller, Chris. (April 16, 2019). "Best Peer-to-Peer Lending Sites for Borrowers and Investors". https://moneyunder30.com/peer-to-peer-lending-sites-for-borrowers-and-investors/

Hayes, Deacon. (March 30, 2019). "80 Easy Ways to Make Money Fast". https://wellkeptwallet.com/best-money-making-ideas/

Chapter 6.

O'Shea, Arielle. (July 25, 2019) "How to Invest in Stocks". https://www.nerdwallet.com/blog/investing/how-to-invest-in-stocks/

Dixon, Amanda. (June 5, 2019). "How CD Laddering Can Help You Boost Your Earnings". https://www.bankrate.com/banking/cds/cd-ladder-guide/

Beattie, Andrew. (Updated May 27, 2019). "4 Simple Ways to Invest in Real Estate". https://www.investopedia.com/investing/simple-ways-invest-real-estate/

www.ingramcontent.com/pod-product-compliance
Lightning Source LLC
Chambersburg PA
CBHW022013120526
44592CB00034B/807